SALLY CLARKE'S BOOK

*Recipes from a restaurant,
shop & bakery*

SALLY CLARKE'S BOOK

Recipes from a restaurant, shop & bakery

FOREWORD BY
Alice Waters

MACMILLAN

First published 1999 by Macmillan
an imprint of Macmillan Publishers Ltd
25 Eccleston Place, London SW1W 9NF
Basingstoke and Oxford
Associated companies throughout the world
www.macmillan.co.uk

ISBN 0 333 74567 1

1 3 5 7 9 8 6 4 2

A CIP catalogue record for this book is available from
the British Library.

Typeset by SX Composing DTP, Rayleigh, Essex
Printed and bound in Great Britain by
Butler & Tanner Ltd, Frome and London

For Samuel

THANK-YOUS

On the endpapers of this book are photographs of the restaurant and shopfront partially obscured by my staff. As I write this, I believe that we at the restaurant, shop, bakery and office number forty-four in total, so we are far too numerous to be named individually.

However, one person in this crowd shines out for me more than any other. She was with me at the conception, with me at the first unlocking of the door, she helped paint the walls and window frames and cleaned up after the builders had finally left. She organized laying the tables for me on the opening night as well as arranging all the flowers, foliage and Christmas decorations, and still to this day (now aged sixty-nineish) she wakes every Monday morning at three thirty, drives to Covent Garden from the country with the car full of foliage and herbs from her garden, chooses our flowers and plants for the week, carries the boxes herself to the car, delivers them to the restaurant and arranges them all, for the individual tables, the kitchen bar, the shop and the lavatories. This wonderful woman, my mother, has been my most constant supporter. Fired with unfailing energy and always smiling, she continues to fill our Mondays with joy and laughter.

Thank you also to Alice Waters who without hesitation agreed to write the foreword for this book even though her busy life is constantly filled with far more important issues and concerns. To Liz Payne, my Head Chef, who keenly accepted the unenviable job of testing each recipe, adding the sensible suggestion that it should be done at her home instead of the restaurant, to reflect domestic kitchen equipment and oven temperatures more accurately, for the benefit of the home cook. To Jill Norman for agreeing to co-edit this book with Macmillan, even though at its outset I am sure to her it seemed like a daunting, if not hopeless, task. To Martin Brigdale for taking so much care over the photographs. To Elaine Hutchings for patiently showing me a hundred times how to move a file from a floppy disk to a hard disk. To Alan Christea for being the epitome of generosity from year one in lending a wondrous selection of art for our walls. To Peter Langan, posthumously, for giving me such sensible and straightforward

architectural and design advice before the builders moved in. To Caradoc King for his encouragement. To Simon Rendall for showing me the importance of getting the look of the book right. To Jonathan Waxman for teaching me how to grill by example. To our numerous suppliers who try so hard on our behalf to produce fruits, vegetables, salads and herbs to such a high standard of excellence. And finally to my husband, John, whose faith in me, constructive criticism and constant, gentle pressure over the years have pushed me to limits I may never have dared to attempt to reach . . .

STAFF PAST & PRESENT

Amongst the faces on the inside covers are some wonderful people who have been with me for what seems like a lifetime.

Julia Devlin, my General Manager and my closest business confidante, has for almost twelve years worked her way to the top of our little tree, and now controls all the finances of each sector of the business and still makes time to discuss with me both the major and minor problems of the day. With her fair-mindedness and patience she has guided me and the business throughout the years. Her poise and gentle but authoritative presence in the restaurant are missed since she now has to spend most of her day in the office glued to the figures on the screen. But on the occasions when extra help is needed in the dining room, she slips into the old routine as if she had never left it.

There is a well-known story of an American tourist speaking to Paul Bocuse during one of his many promotional trips abroad. She enquired of him who cooked whilst he was away from his restaurant. 'Madame,' he replied, 'the same people who cook when I *am* at the restaurant.' I feel the same about Liz Payne, who has been my Head Chef for all but the first of her eleven years with me. As I am no longer a full-time member of the kitchen brigade, confidence in her ability to make decisions in my place is paramount. With ultimate responsibility for both the restaurant and shop production, she oversees all with immaculate attention to detail. As the following photographs will confirm, her skills in presentation are especially enviable and her plates a delight to look at.

Sarah Dickinson has been the Restaurant Manager for the majority of her years at Clarke's, having taken over from Julia in 1994. Sarah's upward progress through the ranks of the restaurant has been a great source of pride to me and a great compliment. She began at Clarke's as a waitress and, having been constantly praised for her speed and efficiency, was made Assistant to Julia. Sarah now divides her time between the dining room and the office, where she takes care of the wages, the maintenance, dining room staff schedules, their training and welfare. With her logical mind she seems to get it all done with consummate ease.

England. From its improvisatory and amateurish beginnings, by remaining curious, honest, and lively, Chez Panisse grew into a force for change in the American diet, as it has always tried to demonstrate that the best meals are composed of seasonal ingredients, for the most part local, which have been sustainably harvested and organically grown, on a small scale; prepared by hand, freshly and simply, and hospitably and beautifully served.

Sally Clarke has been driven by the same impulses. She had similar experiences in her years of passionate study abroad and exactly the same sources of inspiration: writers like Elizabeth David and Richard Olney, and retaurants like Au Pactole and Il Vipore. One time she sent me a letter on the olive oil stained brown paper bag menu from Il Vipore near Lucca filled with rosemary that they had served with the fried potatoes. Like me, she fell in love with the idea of offering her guests an ever-changing, composed menu of several courses, with no choices; and when she opened Clarke's, she became the only admirer of Chez Panisse to actually adopt this format, our most idiosyncratic feature, but which I think has had an amazing educational effect on our diners over the years. She has struggled to build and maintain a network of artisanal suppliers who operate in ecologically sound ways, and her knowledge and understanding of food is deeply informed by these relationships. People who know Chez Panisse well will immediately recognize Clarke's as a restaurant in the same spirit, but with an identity that is uniquely its own because of the local sources and its food and Sally's own special aesthetic.

As this splendid book makes clear, Sally Clarke is always thinking about how to please people. (She has never let me board a flight out of London without making sure I had something delicious to eat. One time I mentioned I had particularly liked a pâté at dinner and she went back to the restaurant in the middle of the night and surprised me early in the morning with a picnic basket containing not only the pâté, but the thinnest slices of her best smoked salmon, perfectly ripe figs wrapped in damp linen napkins, bread and cheese, and a pain au chocolat – the best I've ever had – for my daughter.) This book is both a record of her success, and a guidebook for the reader to do likewise. May it inspire you with its authority, its authenticity, and its vitality.

Alice Waters
Berkeley, California

CONTENTS

INTRODUCTION

The Beginning

From the early 1960s my family's summer holidays were spent largely in France. My parents would fill our car with buckets and spades and suitcases and drive my two brothers and me to Portsmouth or Dover to board the ferry. Normally we would have booked a small hotel for our first night and after that had an approximate route mapped out to our final destination. The discoveries made in between planted the seed of adventure and curiosity about food in me.

As we drove through Normandy and Brittany taking the (then very) small N roads, we would stop in village shops to buy fruit, pâtés, cheeses and breads for our picnic lunches. The array of foods in the shops and markets was staggering to me even then. Why were the fruits so ripe and plentiful? The peaches could be peeled just by looking at them and apricots had a vivid sharpness of flavour and such juiciness. There were tiny malformed discoloured fruits looking like squashed strawberries that had such a heady scent that I was desperate to know what they were. Fraises de bois, unknown to me then and so strange, have become now one of my very favourite fruits.

It was here, in France, that we learned how to eat an artichoke leaf by leaf, dipping and swirling each one into the vinaigrette, sucking the end and laying the denuded leaves on one side.

We tried mussels, clams and langoustines. Calf's brains in a puff-pastry case were served at one of the little hotels and I can still remember the melting creaminess of their texture. My parents, probably wisely, did not explain to us fully the exact contents of that meal until later that evening, but as a result I was never afraid of trying anything new. We were brought up to taste each and every different food in a relaxed and natural way and that has been the basis of my learning and understanding of the table, its food and wine.

By ten or eleven years of age I was cooking at home with my mother. We would read her paperback copies of Elizabeth David's books together and then attempt to create a dish for which we had the ingredients. Soon I was attempting

Sunday lunch by myself whilst my parents and brothers busied themselves in the garden. I was at my happiest in the kitchen, or in the dining room laying the table or serving the dish to my family.

From the age of thirteen I worked for pocket money in my school holidays for a caterer in my home town, Guildford in Surrey. It was here that I learned that work in a kitchen involved long and hard hours, but I loved it and I longed for the next holiday to arrive so that I could work at another wedding or cocktail party or dinner party. I learned to make four pints of béchamel sauce (as I explained to my mother later, 'in one go') and how to wash lettuces by the dozen without crushing them and to cut off the tops of vol-au-vent cases without damaging the edges. A few years later I was trusted enough by the same caterer, Jean Alexander, to arrange dishes at buffet parties with her. Apart from hard work, she taught me about presentation and that garnishes should be bold. A whole bunch of watercress on the side of a platter of Coronation chicken was appropriate, not one tiny sprig of English parsley which, in the 70s, had become the accepted style. Jean was a confident, organized and competent cook and I was exceptionally fortunate to have worked for her at that time.

After school I studied for two years at Croydon Technical College. The course was entitled Hotel and Catering Operations but involved such diverse subjects as Cooking, Baking, Cake Decoration, Hotel Accommodation, Wine and Dining Room Service, Science, Accountancy and Law. I enjoyed and benefited from this basic but thorough course, which was led by dedicated tutors, some of whom I have retained as friends and have become customers.

In some ways, however, I was a difficult student, demanding in lesson one for example that I should be allowed to place a mint sprig instead of a glacé cherry on my grapefruit half. I had by then already become accustomed to the use of more natural ingredients and less traditional presentations and a glacé cherry was the last thing on my mind with which to decorate my grapefruit. I nevertheless left college with a happy heart if not exceptional grades, and presented myself at the Cordon Bleu school in Paris for a three-month advanced course in cooking and baking.

In many ways this course was a repeat performance of that at Croydon. The methods of cooking were again rooted in the classical French tradition, the ingredients were more extravagant and varied, but essentially I was being taught the same lessons more expensively. The great advantage was being in Paris. Here I could walk through street markets brimming with the spring fruits and

vegetables. I could peer in through restaurant windows and marvel at the polished glass and brass and study the beautiful script of handwritten menus. With my mostly American friends from the school I would sit in cafés reading the *Herald Tribune* and sip little cups of coffee, eat Croques Monsieur at grubby tables and ice creams and sorbets from Bertillon on the Île St-Louis.

In order to sustain my life in Paris further, once I had completed the course I decided to find daytime work in a restaurant and also look for a family who required a cook in lieu of payment for accommodation. This I found in the form of a kind American-French family of five living in the rue du Passy, all unfortunately on diets. Nevertheless I moved in to the empty maid's room on the sixth floor and cooked simple light dishes for them each evening during the week. At the weekends I would leave the 16th and go to the 5th, 6th and 7th arrondissements for a more bohemian life. Here my friends and I would pass the morning spending what little cash we had in the markets, butchers' shops, wine merchants and fishmongers, all afternoon in one of their kitchens preparing the feast, and all evening happily consuming it.

During the weekdays, however, I was hard at unpaid work. Raymond Oliver, the owner of Le Grand Vefour in the Palais Royal, generously granted me an interview without notice, and allowed me to explain why I so wanted to learn how to cook in a professional kitchen with paying customers on the other side of the kitchen wall. He agreed with me and suggested that I speak to his son, who owned a large restaurant on the left bank, Le Bistrot de Paris. The following week I was slicing onions and chopping herbs for his chef, Pierre Vedel, and although a girl in a French kitchen was almost unheard of then, let alone an English one, I was accepted by him and allowed to learn along with the rest of his brigade.

After three months I was introduced to another restaurant, Au Pactole, and its strict but fair Chef-Patron Jacques Manière. Here the style of cuisine was very different and the seating capacity small.

M. Manière worked himself very hard and was a passionate, dedicated cook. I was reprimanded by him more than by any other chef. My shallots were not diced finely enough, my mushrooms not brushed thoroughly enough. Equally he found me wasteful. My trimmings in the mushroom basket were far too many and I received a gentle clip around the ear for that. But he was equally kind and generous with his time and as a result I have only fond memories of him. On my last day, I remember he wished me well and good luck by slapping my backside so hard that I left the front door almost flying.

The third and final restaurant to generously take me on as a *commis* was Le Recamier, which still exists with its founding owner, Jacques Cantegrit. Here I learned much about shellfish and seafood. My memories of this kitchen are filled with the sight of baskets of langoustines, lobsters, oysters and mussels being delivered by rosy-cheeked men in dark blue overalls and enormous rubber boots. Here I learned how to boil lobsters and to crack the shells without damaging the meat within and to open oysters in a matter of seconds with the knife angled correctly and my hand protected for safety.

That year in Paris was a privilege, a joy and the first stage of what I now know to be a learning curve. I knew that I still had a great deal to see and learn, but blind youthfulness was my arsenal, and with this I felt perfectly equipped to instruct the world on the fine art of the kitchen. My first idea was to become a writer. I wrote (probably illegibly) reams of pages to people who I felt could advise me in achieving this aim. Within these pages I boasted about my long and varied career, my vast list of achievements and my wish to spread my profound knowledge.

Elizabeth David was my first choice to burden with my request. I had spent most of my childhood reading about her travels, her stories of visits to restaurants, their meals of exquisite simplicity and her recipes for reinventing these dishes at home. Having later had the good fortune to know Mrs David, I am sure that she immediately saw through my boasting. There was enthusiasm in my words, and a genuine passion for food, but I am sure that it was plain to her then that I did not possess anything like the necessary foundation or the skills for a career in writing. She could have so easily discarded the letter. Instead, a few weeks later the telephone rang. Elizabeth David spoke to me for what seemed like hours and I was almost speechless throughout. She did not try to dissuade me from pursuing my idea. She suggested instead that I write and write and send the manuscripts to various publications. I would receive refusal after refusal but one day, she explained, one might be accepted. Then, she said sweetly, you will have become a writer. Within a few months, however, I had started to acknowledge my inadequacies, perhaps by reading between the lines of my conversation with Mrs David, or perhaps by realizing that my leaning towards cooking was far greater than that towards a typewriter.

Meanwhile, my cooking career continued under the auspices of Prudence Leith, first at her catering company, where I worked as an assistant cook for over a year, and then as a teacher at Leith's School of Food and Wine in London.

Then one day, out of the blue, one of my American friends from the Cordon Bleu telephoned from California. He was soon to open a restaurant in Malibu and needed support in the kitchen and dining room. Would I go and help him? Silly question. Within two months I had arranged my trip via New York, where I was to work for a short time teaching cookery in a private house, to pay for my onward journey.

I shall never forget arriving in the intense Los Angeles heat, dressed in a thick wool dress and thick brown woolly tights. My friend and his brother, dressed in almost nothing, picked me up from the plane in an ancient open Mustang car and I immediately felt desperately old fashioned and frumpy. But within hours I had rid myself of my London wardrobe and was swimming in the Pacific ocean frantically trying to blend into the California beach life. It nevertheless took me at least a year to acclimatize to this strange country, its people and their way of life, but once I had adjusted I did not want to leave.

Working in Michael McCarty's restaurant, Michael's, in Santa Monica covered the longest stretch of my learning curve. This was the first restaurant I was involved in from its conception. It was 1979 and for Los Angeles the opening of Michael's was like taking a deep breath and inhaling fresh air for the first time. His sunken garden seating area at the rear of the building, filled with mature trees and shrubs, was electronically covered over with canvas when necessary. The dining-room walls were liberally covered with artworks by David Hockney, Frank Stella and Richard Diebenkorn, and vases of arum lilies filled the air with their heavy scent. In the kitchen, Jonathan Waxman was creating what was soon to be named Californian cooking. Lime-marinated raw slices of fish with leaves of coriander, expertly filleted meats and fish, char-grilled with lightness of touch, finished with extravagant sauces made with sweet Wisconsin butter or white truffles imported from Italy. For dessert, James Brinkley and Nancy Silverton prepared a sideboard daily which displayed vividly coloured glazed fruit tarts, mousses and dark and white chocolate cakes. It was a break-away style much needed in Los Angeles at a time when the culinary choice was little more than the 1950s style red-leather boothed American steak house, or classic French food served under silver domes on basketweave Villeroy and Boch plates. Of course both had their place and both were successful but Michael's was different and I stayed for more than four years, learning first-hand about creating and running a restaurant.

But by the end of 1983 I was missing what I remembered fondly as 'normal' life. To me living in California was like a dream; perfect weather, very special friends, a privileged lifestyle but one which sadly was not real. However much I tried, I continued to feel like a foreigner. It was time to go home and to put my ideas into practice.

One year later Clarke's Restaurant opened, and although I feel that London is now home I sometimes desperately miss my friends in America, and the restaurants, vineyards and bakeries. To compensate, I try to visit them at least once a year, not only to keep in touch with the people but also to feed off their inspiration, their enthusiasm and knowledge. I find as much inspiration in their menus and markets as I do by travelling to Europe, sometimes more. Alice Waters' restaurant, Chez Panisse, is still my favoured touchstone, where I often book lunch, dinner, lunch, dinner, over a two-day stay in the San Francisco area. There is still so much for me to absorb and learn there.

Inspiration

To me many British restaurant menus in the 60s and 70s seemed too long, too complicated and too full of inappropriate ingredients for the season. Some restaurant menus never seemed to change from year to year. The gravy-splattered card on which they were printed was proof to that. What a joy it was to go instead to unpretentious out-of-the-way restaurants, in France or Italy for example, where the menus were often written on a blackboard, or freshly hand-written on a card in the window. Or even better, where the menu was given verbally at the table by the patron, as at the restaurant Vipore, just outside Lucca in Tuscany, or Da Noi in Florence, both sadly now closed, which took great pride in planning menus around their garden or neighbourhood farmers' market respectively. Those amongst very few others were inspiration to me as I was forming my plans for Clarke's.

Without any doubt at all, however, it was my first visit to Chez Panisse in Berkeley, California in 1979 that set my wayward ideas into a semblance of order. As I was served a perfectly balanced no-choice dinner menu, Alice Waters flitted in and out of the kitchen with dishes of herb-marinated lentils, baked peppers with salted anchovies, spit-roasted pigeons and exquisite salad leaves tossed in olive oil and shallots. Sitting in Chez Panisse that evening, I soaked up as much as I possibly could: its atmosphere, its decor, the tablecloths, the baskets of hedgerow flowers on the side tables alongside the bowls of tomatoes and aubergines. I also noted the way in which the dining-room staff conducted themselves. Without any sense of superiority, even though they knew how privileged they were to be working there, they moved amongst the tables with grace and ease. The pride with which the waitress carried a bottle of wine to the table was as if her father had picked the grapes himself, and the way in which the plates were placed on the table was with careful confidence.

Even though I had arrived in America only a few months before, I had heard about Alice Waters. She was and still is the best-known woman restaurateur in America and this is the favoured restaurant for those who simply love food for its own sake, without the pomp and circumstance normally associated with long-established American restaurants. At Chez Panisse, Alice creates an inspired way of hospitality.

With her unique generosity of spirit, she offers to her customers ingredients which have been grown or reared in an organic or ecological manner. She nurtures and encourages farmers and gardeners to produce goods to her specifications and then uses them in a simple and unfussy way to show them at their best. Without question it was Alice who gave me the confidence to try this somewhat crazy no-choice idea for myself five years later in London, and it is she who continues to be my most important source of inspiration to do better and to try harder.

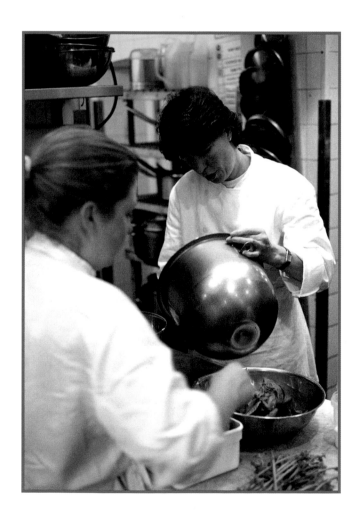

The Opening of the Restaurant

From my teenage years I had bored my family stiff with my vision of a restaurant which would offer a set menu in the evenings planned solely around the best, the freshest and the most seasonal of products presented in a wholesome and healthy way. It would include salads, tossed with fruity olive oils and herbs; marinated and grilled meats and fish with simple garnishes; vegetables carefully prepared and only *just* cooked, retaining their colour, texture and nutrients. British and Irish cheeses would be included, specially chosen by the cheesemakers themselves, and served at the peak of ripeness to display the range and diversity of their craft. Desserts would be produced with small amounts of sugar to allow the fruits, pastries and creams to show their own distinct flavours and sweetness.

At lunch the format would be slightly different. Although still changing daily, the menu would offer a small choice of dishes reflecting the highlights in the market on the day.

Although many people were supportive of the idea, most were frightened for me. This was after all a bizarre if not crazy idea, destined for failure. I distinctly remember one friend saying that of course they understood what I meant by no choice, 'But surely you will offer a *small* choice as well, won't you?'

The argument was that it is accepted that at a friend's dinner party one is not offered a choice, but there one does not have to pay. Nevertheless, I insisted that at Clarke's it would be different, and now, fifteen years later, hardly a day goes by when I do not thank my very lucky star that there is continued desire on the part of our loyal customers to return time and time again to put their faith and trust in us, to present what we believe to be a perfectly balanced, carefully thought-out menu, reflecting the best of the season.

The opening of Clarke's Restaurant, Kensington Church Street on 17 December 1984 was a quiet and rather discreet affair without the aid of publicity or a PR machine. The first night was as planned, albeit two months later than I had hoped. The dining room was filled with invited family and friends. Served by a handful of young, willing waiting staff, the kitchen brigade of two prepared and presented a set no-choice menu of four courses: a salad of smoked salmon, watercress, avocado and pink grapefruit followed by grilled rosemary-marinated chump chop of lamb, then a selection of cheeses, and for dessert crème brûlée with poached rhubarb. My memories of the evening are vague, probably due to the exhaustion from negotiating with the landlords, builders, architects, planning officers, fire department and building inspectors. Collectively they had created a tired and emaciated (but nevertheless ecstatically happy) restaurateur. Visions of smoke billowing up the stairs from a kitchen struggling with an inefficient extractor system and the resulting streaming eyes is one memory I have of that night. Our modest attempt at Christmas decoration was a beautiful branch of contorted willow which stood by the door festooned with silver tinsel ribbons, but these were blown off in the draught as the first guests arrived, leaving the branch completely naked but for a pile of tinsel wrapped around its ankle on the floor. The downstairs dining room was still a building site, as one with the kitchen, with the bar which would eventually divide the two lying in a hundred pieces on the floor awaiting assembly.

Happily we were able to serve up to thirty customers a night over the Christmas week, before we had to close again to finish the building works completely. That took another three weeks, but at least we had managed to open at a time when guests were in a happy and relaxed frame of mind and willing to forgive the minor – and sometimes major – inconveniences. It was a time when my family and friends were the only customers and major source of support. They were there every night, bringing different guests, introducing new people to the style of food and service and being the most generous ambassadors of The Restaurant That Had No Choice.

At last the idea which had been growing within me since the age of fourteen had been born. I had proved to family and friends, and most importantly to myself, that I was capable of creating something as complex as a restaurant, without the help of a business partner or outside investor other than my darling father whose financial help bridged the gap between the bank and me.

I had chosen the light fittings, the chairs, the pots and pans and the layout of the kitchen, the paint colour on the walls and the wood on the floor. I had spent weeks speaking to suppliers of kitchen equipment, china, glassware and cutlery. In the absence of an office, I had even conducted my interviews with prospective staff in the privacy of the ladies' lavatory, as this had been the only peaceful corner, away from the electric saws and pneumatic drills.

I was convinced that the style of the restaurant should be modern though not fashionable, that it should be full of daylight but not garishly bright. I wanted it to feel comfortable but not plush, and that an immediate feeling of freshness and simplicity would be obvious to anyone walking through the door.

I did not want a 'decorated' feel to the rooms. Instead I wished the style to be understated, and to a large degree this feeling has been sustained over the years, and the fabric and decor of the rooms have changed little.

The format of the menus, reflecting ideas I had explored for many years, has not changed either: a seasonal no-choice dinner menu each evening, comprising four courses, and a daily changing lunch menu with a small selection of dishes have been offered since day one. My reasons for this format were simple. At night I felt we would attract more customers who were entertaining for family or social reasons and who therefore would perhaps be in a more comfortable frame of mind to explain any allergy or dietary problem with the menu. In contrast it was likely that the vast majority of our lunchtime custom would be meeting for business, and therefore perhaps not necessarily known to each other. In order to save embarrassment to host or guest it seemed best to offer a small choice, thus allowing the flexibility of menu to take account of their dietary preferences.

But most of all, I wanted the menus to reflect the qualities and variations of

the seasons. They would be constructed around the best and freshest of the market on that day, the dinner menus especially being perfectly balanced to enable the diner to taste a number of different ingredients with various flavours and textures, and to allow him or her to complete the meal without feeling either bloated or unsatisfied.

Moving Into Next Door

Three years later the building next door to the restaurant, a launderette, became vacant. At that stage we were turning away customers more often than we had spare tables, and the staff changing room had shrunk due to the increase in personnel. My 'office' was a corner of the kitchen and the manager's was a table in the dining room. In those days fifty per cent of our customers wore fur coats in the winter and our coat room was understandably bulging under the strain. It was time to expand. The launderette building was purchased along with a sitting tenant in the flat above, and the builders moved in. We closed for three months to do the work, which was very optimistic on the part of the architects, but we

managed. The wall in the basement dividing the two buildings was removed, air-conditioning was installed and new customer lavatories were added. The staff room was designed to fit into a tight corner but at least now everyone had room to hang their belongings. The kitchen, which was also extended, retained the open-plan view of the dining room across the bar, and was stretched sideways giving more storage space, a well-planned wash-up area and a greater amount of room for preparation and service work. New kitchen equipment was lowered into the basement through the floor of the old launderette, which had been removed totally due to damp.

One of these pieces of equipment was a large bread oven, bought specifically to allow us the opportunity of 'bottom baking' our bread instead of baking in tins or on baking sheets. In this way we could bake our hand-shaped bread flat on the hot tiles of the oven base, thus adding a more professional dimension to our baking.

The building's outside appearance changed slightly also with a more stylish shopfront which included bevelled glass windows and dark green paintwork. Although many regular customers were initially nervous that the original personality and charm of the restaurant would be lost by its expansion, we were able to prove this was not the case.

The dining rooms were more spacious and more comfortable, the stainless steel cutlery had been replaced by silverware and our (mostly borrowed) selection of contemporary art had expanded, along with the extra wall space, and most importantly the chefs were able to produce an even wider range of dishes due to the increased kitchen area and the fact that we had redesigned its layout to our own specifications. Within a few weeks of the restaurant reopening, our shop next door opened its doors in April 1988. The shop was called & Clarke's, a confusing if not puzzling name to many of our customers, but I felt that it was the simplest name for a shop which was linked to the restaurant next door. From the street, of course, the names joined together perfectly, forming the names of the combined businesses, Clarke's & Clarke's.

Although neither my staff nor I possessed any retail experience, it seemed timely to open a shop to sell our baked goods, along with cheeses from Neal's Yard Dairy, Californian wines and our chocolate truffles, as for years our restaurant customers had requested bread, oatmeal biscuits or truffles, or all three, to take home after their meal.

What could be more ideal than to have bread baked on the premises, carried up the stairs in wicker baskets and sold as it cooled to the local Kensington population?

Within a few years (and I fully admit it took that long) we had begun to understand the basics of retailing, and along with the range of goods which we offered our customer base started to expand. Wholesale customers such as Monmouth Coffee House and Neal's Yard Dairy added to the demand. At the same time we began producing jams, pickles, chutneys, marinated olives, cakes, sweet and savoury tarts, pizza and focaccia in the restaurant kitchens and we found that the more we put in the shop the more our patrons demanded. I soon discovered that although a customer might arrive through the door with the

sole purpose of buying one walnut loaf, quite often, before leaving, they would have chosen enough items to fill two carrier bags! More recently we have added a display refrigerator which houses our pots of daily made soups, sauces, relishes and juices. Organically produced fruits, vegetables and herbs are now an everyday feature, arranged in baskets, reflecting the menu ideas from next door with immediacy.

The great success of the shop led on to the sad but inevitable expulsion of our baker from the restaurant kitchens. Even though he started work at midnight, as the chefs were leaving the kitchen, and finished his shift as the pastry chefs arrived in the early morning, he was producing too many loaves and required too much space for us all to live happily together.

In 1990 a small building in North Kensington was found which we transformed into a well-equipped and well-designed environment for us to create our wholesale business, which of course had to be named & Clarke's Bread. Within weeks a van had been purchased and a delivery service was offered to our handful of customers within central London. By 1997 we were producing enough bread for over thirty restaurant, hotel, coffee bar and speciality food shop customers and the staff at the bakery had grown to ten. At the same time the chocolate truffle and biscuit production had been transferred there from the restaurant kitchen. It was time again for us to find larger premises.

& Clarke's Bread is now housed in a larger more modern North Kensington building and produces twenty-five different types of bread, rolls, croissants and brioche on a seven nights a week basis, using traditional methods of hand shaping and bottom baking. During the daytime, sweet and savoury tart shells are rolled and chilled ready for transportation to the restaurant, where they are filled with an ever-increasing variety of ingredients to sell in the shop. Our special granola and muesli recipes are made and packaged there also along with spiced nuts, sugared almonds and the sweet, savoury and oatmeal biscuits.

MENU PLANNING

Our Suppliers

Quite obviously growing vegetables, fruits, salads and herbs in Britain does not have the advantages of climate offered for example by southern Europe and California, but I was convinced that in some small way we at Clarke's could progress along a route of sourcing as many ingredients as possible from British producers. I felt that at the very least we could try to offer our customers carefully grown and beautifully prepared and presented food from the gardens of Britain almost year-round.

From the outset, the menus have been planned around what the vegetable market dictated. I talk to my suppliers constantly to reap the benefit of their knowledge of what is in perfect condition and in season. In the beginning the style of the restaurant menus tended to be 'English' and 'safe'. I used very little coriander, chilies, raw fish dishes, shellfish or game and tended to keep well within the boundaries of familiar ingredients and familiar presentations. This suited our then predominantly central London clientele but very soon, with the aid of favourable reviews both from home and abroad, we attracted a wider audience and our menus became more confident and varied.

For many years now they have been firmly rooted in Mediterranean influences; lots of olive oil, herbs, salads and lightly cooked vegetables. Grilled meats and fish, as in our early days, are still an important part of our style, but roasting, poaching and braising have evolved as almost equal partners.

It is interesting to note that at Clarke's, along with orders for gin and tonics, the demand for red meats has gently decreased over the years. I do not believe that this is necessarily a reflection on the emergence of Creutzfeldt-Jakob disease, as we have always proudly displayed on the menu the fact that we buy only from farms which raise their cattle under traditional, ecologically sound methods. Rather I feel that there is a general leaning towards lighter, more easily digestible foods, and this preference is most noticeable at lunch, where, given a choice of dishes, our customers prefer fish or white-fleshed meats such as rabbit, chicken and guinea fowl.

In the evening, I tend to favour these items also for the dinner menus, with fish often playing the main course role on three out of the five nights. Vegetarian dishes including cheeses such as buffalo mozzarella, ricotta, fresh goat or Parmesan form many of our first courses as well as smoked fish salads, thinly sliced San Daniele ham and various pasta dishes. The third course has always been the same: a selection of British or Irish cheeses served with oatmeal biscuits and unsalted butter accompanied by a little pile of breakfast radishes or a piece of celery heart. It has never worried me that the menu often has two courses including cheese, as our cheeses are all so varied in style, texture, flavour and strength that it is almost like serving a completely different food altogether.

Throughout this book, cheeses are suggested as a separate course, usually accompanied by oatmeal biscuits, fruit, a salad or radishes, freshly cracked nuts or toasts. They are placed in the menus purely as suggestions and although at the restaurant we use a combination of two or three cheeses, it may make your menus even more special if just one cheese is chosen at its peak of ripeness and correct for the season. I prefer to eat the softer cheeses in the summer, such as young goat's or cow's milk cheese; Tymsboro, Innes, or Finn. Cashel Blue, Wigmore and

Croghan are also perfect, served with bunches of cherries or peppery radishes with their leaves still attached or figs and apricots. When the cooler autumn and winter months arrive, the fuller flavoured cheeses such as the Cheddars, Stilton, Lancashire, Gubbeen, Cheshire and Berkswell seem to complement and balance the richer foods. Nevertheless I still feel that a good sharp apple or pear or celery heart is necessary to cut the richness of the cheese with perhaps the addition of a slice of hazelnut and raisin or wholemeal bread.

I would never dream of going into a shop armed with a list of ingredients for a pre-planned menu. Equally I never reflect on past menus to gain inspiration for future ones as I am convinced that the available products of the day or of the week are inspiration enough to guide even a beginner or amateur cook to provide a meal composed of appropriate ingredients. The simplest menu, such as a

selection of cheeses and a salad, can be uplifting and satisfying if prepared and presented in a thoughtful and careful way.

Over the years we have come to know a small handful of very special farmers and gardeners who work with us in providing a wonderful array of ingredients. From purple figs grown on a south-facing wall of a mid-eighteenth century walled garden in the heart of Suffolk to courgette blossoms and wild rocket from a raggedy field just off the M25 in Surrey to twenty different types of pumpkins and squash from Southampton to nasturtium blossoms and leaves picked from a garden in Kent, we have been blessed with the products of our suppliers' hard work and dedication. It is they, in essence, who plan the menus for me and they who allow us, the cooks, to perform.

Each week, normally at the weekend, I fulfil my role at the restaurant as menu planner. This primarily involves telephoning our suppliers and discussing the availability of their products, whether they be fruit, vegetable, fish, meat, salad or herb. I listen to their joys as they speak of their successes and to their frustrations over unhelpful weather or their misbehaving farm equipment. As they speak I list their suggestions at the top of my page and mark each suggestion with either the day of its proposed picking or landing at port or the day on which their delivery would ideally be made. That is the easy part. Then comes the job of collating their suggestions in such a way that allows each ingredient to show itself to its full potential and in its best light. At the same time I attempt to create dishes that are appropriately assembled and which will balance each other in a menu. It is important also that each and every component of a meal can be recognized. For this reason our dishes are never complicated. Awareness of colours, textures and flavours is essential.

The weight and density of each dish should take equal importance. For example, a menu which incorporates cream, eggs, fats and carbohydrates at every stage might well suit a greedy person (and some people I know), but would probably not appeal to people more concerned about their health and wellbeing. At the end of a meal I want our customers to feel comfortable and still able to enjoy one of our hand-rolled bitter chocolate truffles, which are offered with coffee.

The cooking at Clarke's is simple, without gimmicks or fiddling. The hard part of our style is in the buying, the attention to detail in its preparation, the care with which ingredients are handled and the spirit in which we place the food on the plate.

The Seasons

To me the perfect way to compile a menu is first to wander through a local vegetable garden or a farmers' market in France, Italy or California and choose the ingredients by their merit, their look, their smell and their feel. Sadly, for the restaurant we do not yet have the luxury of many such markets in London and the south east. Instead, in our search for the best we enlist the help of private gardeners and farmers who are able to produce goods on our behalf.

Over the years I have become increasingly aware of the need to seek out the producers who work in an ecological if not organic way. At Clarke's we have had the good fortune of being able to do this by sourcing ingredients for the menus from many British specialist growers who understand the importance of sustainable agriculture. Some have been recommended to us by other restaurants, some have just introduced themselves, some are friends of friends, but what they all have in common is a passion for their product and a pride in the wholesome way they produce their goods. I could easily buy all my fruit and vegetable ingredients year round from Covent Garden market if I wished, but there one has to assume that the vast majority of goods are produced by intensive farming methods on a large scale where profit, not necessarily ecology, is the main aim. Although I openly admit having to buy some items from the market every day, most predominantly during the winter months, we have been able to source an increasing number of ingredients from individuals who work within traditional methods to produce goods which taste, feel and look like the real thing. It gives us a tremendous sense of pride to write the name of the grower or producer on the menu as this helps to create an awareness amongst our customers of the quality of their work.

Even though we categorize our year by its seasons there are in every year grey areas as one season blends into the next, or in some extraordinary cases even reverts to the previous one. Some seasons fool us into thinking that we have moved way ahead of the norm and into a season alien to its month. No one is more aware of this than the gardeners, and it is to them that I turn primarily for guidance. We rely heavily on their word that something is at its peak and should be bought. Very rarely are we disappointed; our regular suppliers know us well now.

The simplest way for me to create a picture of the range of vegetable, herb and fruit produce as it evolves over the year is by reading our kitchen orders diary.

As I turn over the pages of last year's orders I can see the ebb and flow of the seasons clearly. The winter months seem interminably long. It is at this time of year that the carrots and cabbages seem endless, but our British suppliers are nevertheless still bursting with stored apples and pears. The frosts have started to help in the production of healthy Savoy and red cabbages, Brussels sprouts, both red- and green-leaved curly kale, some varieties of broccoli and of course many root vegetables – Jerusalem artichokes, salsify, celeriac and parsnips.

From the south-west of France the true black truffle is arriving late in the year as well as supplies of beautiful bitter-leaved salad greens such as trevisse, Belgian endive and pissenlit (dandelion). The citrus fruits from southern Europe are starting to peak around November; clementines, mandarins, both thick- and thin-skinned oranges and the sharp Seville oranges start their relatively short season. Some stored quince are still filtering through from Turkey and Greece, and by Christmas if we are lucky the blood oranges from Spain start to arrive.

By the new year we are buying toffee dates from California and Egyptian pink garlic but it is not really until March or April when the spring produce arrives that we see a vast difference in the range of goods. Jersey Royal potatoes

are probably the first indication of this: embedded in a light sprinkling of soil, they arrive from the market in little wooden caskets. If we are very lucky a few morel mushrooms from Scotland may trickle in. Wild and garden rocket which has been growing in plastic tunnels is being picked in Surrey as well as pea shoots, Swiss chard, leaf broccoli, sorrel and corn salad. Spring artichokes are imported from France and the best forced rhubarb comes to us from Yorkshire. April also means the start of the asparagus. Grown in East Anglia, it is the only green asparagus that I consider using as to me imported asparagus bears no resemblance to the real thing either in appearance or taste. By mid-June the asparagus beds are put to rest for another year so we use as much as we can in as many ways during that peak time. From Sicily, organic lemons and different varieties of blood oranges with their leaves still attached are arriving by mid-April and we start to sell them both in the shop as well as in the restaurant. May brings us the ugly but exquisitely perfumed Alphonse mangoes from India.

We start to buy the first of the French strawberries in June. I never consider the weather to be warm enough much before then to place soft fruit on the menus, but it is not long after this that the British strawberries then raspberries then

currants appear, and our menus are filled with summer berry desserts. English peas and broad beans are with us by mid-June and the stone fruits from France are usually worth buying by early July. By then the white, blush-red and yellow peaches, apricots and nectarines are so perfect in ripeness and flavour that they beg to be used. The short season of summer truffles from France and Spain starts in early July. English cherries of all the different colours, usually from Kent or Sussex, have a relatively short season also but we use them to the limit in both the shop and restaurant along with gooseberries, redcurrants and blackcurrants.

From July courgettes, often with their blossom attached, are delivered almost daily to us from Surrey with sheaves of rocket, both wild and garden, young spinach, landcress, mizuna and three basils: bush, purple and Genovese. From Wiltshire we receive three different types of organic beetroot, plum tomatoes, young leeks and young fennel, the size of a fat thumb.

Even though vine tomatoes are arriving from Italy thick and fast by June, I do not consider June to be a tomato month. I prefer to hold out and wait until July when, if all goes well, the central London heat is becoming oppressive and our customers are crying out for the refreshingly sharp salads and soups of tomatoes. The real extra-fine French beans (haricots verts) are picked from July in France and although I admit to buying their not-so-slim cousin from Kenya at times during the rest of the year, there is really no comparison with the real thing.

August sees the emergence of another organic supplier, this time from Southampton. He specializes in dozens of different types of pumpkin and squash in the autumn months but also grows yellow and purple beans, beetroot of various colours, tiny vine tomatoes of all shapes and colours, finger aubergines and yellow, red and green chard. By September the English corn on the cob has ripened and a friend in Suffolk is starting to deliver to us the products of his garden: more varieties of tomatoes, shallots, yellow and pale green courgettes, Linzer Delicatesse potatoes and mulberries, and his flowering mint, marjoram and thyme is by now in serious competition with my mother's selection. His purple figs, bursting with ripeness, as bulbous and heavy as pears, are delivered to us wrapped individually by their leaves. October and November see the coming of the British crops of wild mushrooms, ceps, brown and yellow chanterelles, hedgehog mushrooms, and of course the white truffles from Italy. From Kent, apples of many kinds arrive from one of our favourite foragers including Falstaff, Bramley, Gala, and Cox, and the Conference and Comice pears. From Suffolk, some small misshapen quince come to us with the last of that supplier's produce for the year.

When buying through Covent Garden, I try to buy produce from within Britain or as close to Britain as possible, France, Spain and Italy being my favoured sources, as in this way I can be almost assured that the goods have not been sitting in airport hangars, trucks or aeroplanes for days on end before they are finally unpacked by us. It is important to me that we receive the produce as immediately as is possible after picking.

There are, however, one or two exceptions to that rule during the winter and early spring months. I will happily accept the most wonderful sharp-sweet pineapples from the Ivory Coast, mangoes from Guatemala and pink grapefruit from Florida, purely for their fresh acidic and cleansing tastes which balance some of the rich cold-weather foods perfectly.

Much of our fish arrives daily from the West Country. Our contact there buys directly from the boats and in this way I can be assured of absolute fresh-ness. We normally speak on a daily basis and always at the weekends, during which time he advises me on which boats are going out when and what they are expecting to catch. With this help I am able to map out an almost certain plan for the week's dinner menus as well as some of the lunch menu items. Because of our keen leaning towards the char grill, there are particular types of fish which we favour more than others. Plaice or lemon sole fillets are often too delicate to char-grill, but firmer fish such as turbot, red mullet, halibut, cod, brill and monkfish are firm enough to cope with its intense heat and our supplier now knows well which fish to suggest and which to avoid.

Our meats, lamb, pork and beef in the main, are sourced by Mr Lidgate in Holland Park, London, who buys only from farms which can guarantee unadulterated methods of cattle rearing.

France is our usual source of corn-fed poultry such as guinea fowl, chicken and squab pigeon, although we have tried long and hard to find a British farmer who is able to rear such a consistently good product in the quantities that we need.

Cheeses have always been one of the restaurant's and shop's primary sources of pride. From the first year we have bought British and Irish cheeses through Neal's Yard Dairy in London, which buys in the main unpasteurized cheeses directly from the farm, usually in an immature state, and then stores them, cares for them during their maturation and then sells them on a retail or wholesale basis.

This 'middle man' method allows the farmers, who are often smallholders, to recoup some of their costs at an early stage in their production, thus assisting in the management of their cash flow.

We have been introduced to many of the dedicated cheesemakers and they have all been without exception passionate artisans of this ancient craft. Most of them own their own herds of cattle or goats or flocks of sheep and many have been producing the same cheese on the same pasture for generations, giving a natural character and a unique flavour to each one. I have been to the depths of County Cork and visited Norman and Veronica Steele and been included in a 'vertical' tasting of six vintages of Millens around their kitchen table. During a visit to Goosnargh, Lancashire, I met Mrs Kirkham, who makes *the* Lancashire. She introduced me to her husband, who was milking the cows, and then showed me into the cheesemaking parlour where baths full of curds were being cut and pressed into the most beautiful cheeses. She told me that they had never had a holiday and had never been to London. Such dedication and love for their life's work made me gasp with admiration. My staff are regularly invited to travel with the Neal's Yard Dairy van to some of the farms on collection days, where they are able to take an active part in and learn first-hand the intricacies of cheesemaking.

Twice a week we receive a delivery of soft, semi-soft, hard and blue cheeses from the Dairy, which we store and display in the shop. Twice daily the shop selects the cheeses for the lunch and dinner menus, based on their ripeness and suitability for the menu.

Vegans and Vegetarians

Because of our restricted menu in the evenings it is necessary for the kitchen to have a selection of alternative ingredients always available for customers who may have a dietary problem with a particular dish. As a policy, the dining room staff check with each table before the first course is ordered that the menu suits everyone. This allows any dietary preferences to be voiced before the dish is prepared. Quite obviously we would never force anyone to eat anything they felt unable to eat.

Vegans allow themselves a diet of only vegetables, pulses, fruits, nuts, leaves and seeds, and foods derived from those ingredients such as oils. They do not eat any dairy products at all. Vegetarians will eat a vegan diet as well as eggs, milk products and cheese made without natural rennet. Both are welcomed to Clarke's as openly and cheerfully as the happy-go-lucky diners who wish simply to be served their meal without even looking at the menu, allowing each dish to arrive as a surprise.

But then there are the not so real vegans and vegetarians, who tend to be the confused and confusing lot.

We have had to deal with many alternative menus over the years, for quite legitimate reasons, from the simple low-fat diet to the no red meat diet, or shell-fish allergies, but when it comes to the not so real vegans and vegetarians our hackles tend to rise. For example, we once served a customer who claimed to be strictly vegan but when it came to the dessert she was more than happy to eat the lemon tart rich in egg yolks and double cream. On one occasion a gentleman telephoned to make a reservation with the request for one of his guests to be served a vegetarian menu. No problem, we replied. But it later transpired that this vegetarian not only ate fish but was also happy with chicken! Another 'vegetarian', demanding to be vegetarian for the entire menu, was more than willing to change her mind when she saw the salad of San Daniele ham arrive at

the table for her friends. Others, perhaps not entirely happy with the sound of the dinner menu, have requested a vegetarian suggestion, but after hearing about the selection of dishes to be offered have changed their minds back again, rapidly becoming unvegetarian, happy to eat pigeon, rabbit, halibut, scallops, you name it. As a result it has become more and more difficult for us to understand the broad diversity of vegans and vegetarians, their fussiness and fickleness.

On the other side of the coin, as a customer, I enjoy choosing vegetarian dishes when visiting other people's restaurants. I was saddened to note that at a well-known country restaurant in Britain only one dish on the entire summer menu was vegetarian. They even boasted a beautiful vegetable and herb garden which was bursting at the borders with every ingredient imaginable. Perhaps it was there just for decoration. On the other hand one of the most wonderful meals I ate two years ago was in Monte Carlo at the Hôtel de Paris, cooked by Frank Cerrutti, Alain Ducasse's head chef. There I chose for a Sunday lunch in spring the following seven-course menu entitled 'les jardins de Provence'. It was expensive but worth every cent and quite simply, exquisite.

Cream of local spring peas with ricotta and Parmesan gnocchi
Warm morel mushrooms with herbs and olive oil
Casserole of Provençal garden vegetables with sliced black truffles,
balsamic vinegar and rock salt
Wild and green asparagus risotto
Selection of perfectly ripe cheeses
Hot poached wild strawberries with mascarpone sorbet
Selection of caramel desserts

This book includes a wide selection of dishes suitable for vegetarians and vegans, shown in the index by † and ‡.

'Allergies'

As a result of an increased number of allergies being reported to us by our customers over the last few years, I have come to the conclusion that to be a doctor specializing in allergy treatments must be one of the most lucrative sides of the medical profession today. It seems that most people are now allergic to something

— and what an extraordinary list of topics they come up with! It is easy to
understand those with high cholesterol levels avoiding eating saturated fats, or
those with delicate digestive systems avoiding onion, garlic, leek . . . but parsley,
beetroot, spinach? I often think that for some people a simple dislike of a food is
more easily described as an allergy. But to me this is purely a psychological allergy.
There are certain dishes we often place on our menus because we love them but
which are not always a natural choice for our customers. However, it is surprising
how many people are happy to change their minds after taking the plunge and
tasting them.

At the restaurant we find from time to time that some customers are unable to
eat certain items on the menus for dietary or allergic reasons. I have never found
this a problem to deal with even if the customer announces the request seconds
before the dish is about to arrive. Nearly all our dishes are cooked to order and it
is therefore simple to create one portion without butter or with a fish alternative to
the meat or whatever the desired result needs to be. What I have found difficult
in the past, however, is customers' fussiness. It seems illogical to me that just
because one has had fish for lunch in the City that it is not desirable to eat it for
dinner also. Equally, I wonder if it is really likely that just because one hated
rhubarb at school twenty years ago that our spring rhubarb, grown by Mr Olroyd
in Yorkshire and poached gently by us in sweet wine, with vanilla pods from
Madagascar, is going to bear any resemblance at all to the school dinner lady's
rhubarb that came out of a tin. What I have passionately wanted, from the
opening day of the restaurant, is that our customers are at least *willing to try*.

It has amazed and thrilled me to see customers eat pigeon for the first time or
raw artichokes or grilled squid or, as in later recipes, smoked eel (see page 100),
raw anchovies (see page 102) or skate (see page 104), and go away happy and
delighted with the taste, and, more importantly, with a willingness to say yes
to it again.

GARNISHES & SEASONING

Garnishes

Whenever a dish is garnished it must be given the respect of an *appropriate* garnish. For example, if a shoulder of lamb has been stuffed and roasted with onion and sage, parsley and thyme, a garnish of a large sprig of sage or Italian parsley would be ideal.

Chervil is one of the loveliest of herbs, soft, fragrant and feminine, and is perfectly matched with a multitude of ingredients, from carrots to crab to chicken to asparagus. It can be tossed into summer or spring salads, chopped and scattered over warm spring vegetables or used as a flavouring for chilled spring and summer soups. But sadly for chervil it seems to be used on a multitude of inappropriate dishes, becoming the signature garnish for many a dish served mostly in Michelin-starred restaurants. I have even witnessed it garnishing a dish of venison sausages with lentils where clearly neither the dish nor the season had any relationship with chervil at all and as a result I felt almost embarrassed for the chervil being there. I could be a little unkind and suggest that in order to receive a Michelin star one first needs to buy bunches and bunches of it throughout the year to garnish each dish!

Italian parsley (sometimes called Greek or Continental parsley) is the only garnish I consider to be appropriate even if it is not contained in the dish. It can be neutral in its look and smell but at the same time can give height and colour to a dish without detracting from the essence of the ingredients underneath.

Throughout this book garnishes are suggested as a final addition to a dish before serving or presentation. This must be done literally seconds before the dish is delivered to the table in order to create the maximum effect of freshness. A garnish should look bold. A tiny sprig of thyme sitting on the top of a pot-roasted pigeon which had been marinated in thyme would look almost as if it had been placed there by mistake, but a spray of thyme with leaves and if possible some thyme flowers, tucked 'under the arm' of the bird, would look eye-catching and confident.

I consider mint to be a suitable decoration for most of our desserts at the restaurant. The top sprig of five or six leaves is picked from the stem and placed on the top or to the side of the dessert and then often dusted with a little icing sugar. The leaves, being dry, catch the sugar as it falls and this produces a simple but pretty effect. The remaining mint leaves are used to make fresh mint teas in the dining room for those customers who prefer not to drink coffee at the end of their meal. A teapot is simply a quarter filled with leaves, boiling water is poured over and it is then allowed to infuse for a few minutes before being served at the table.

With all herbs, we find it advisable to select the garnish from the total bunch first as in this way the best is saved for the finished dish in order to achieve the maximum effect. The rest of the bunch can be stripped of leaves for chopping or leaving whole, depending on its intended use. The stalks are never thrown away – in fact very little is thrown away in our kitchen. They are invaluable for flavouring stocks, soup bases and broths, but it must always be remembered that they should only be added where appropriate. Coriander stalks would not be correct, for example, in a chicken stock destined for a sauce containing red wine, shallots and thyme, but would be perfect in a chili-spiced tomato broth or as a basis for a tomato and roasted red pepper soup.

Seasoning

Salt and freshly ground pepper are placed on each table every lunch and dinner in tiny wooden dishes to allow the customers to reseason their dish if they feel it is required. We use cracked white and black peppercorns mixed together in one and flaked Maldon salt in the other. Two black marks immediately to any customer who helps themselves to these *without* tasting the dish first.

SALT

In the restaurant kitchen salt is used in two different forms: fine sea salt and flaked Maldon sea salt. For cooking we tend to use the fine sea salt as this is easier to judge for measurement and is less expensive.

The Maldon salt, being more expensive, is used in any finished dish which will when served still retain the majority of its unique texture. Dishes which come into this category tend to be those such as salads of leaves or already cooked vegetables. Salads which include raw buffalo mozzarella or fresh ricotta cheese will often be finished with a sprinkling of it as it adds texture and looks pretty without giving an overly salty taste. We often sprinkle it on top of focaccia or breadsticks just before baking. A small pile of Maldon salt flakes can look very appealing, for example, placed to one side of a dish of raw vegetables (radishes, celery and fennel heart) for the diner to dip into.

If the king of the seasoning list can be afforded, the damp grains of the real *fleur de sel* (sea salt) will add an even further dimension to these recipes.

If on the other hand Maldon salt flakes cannot be afforded, fine sea salt will work just fine.

PEPPER

Twice daily the kitchen grinds a mixture of white and black peppercorns in a small electric grinder. This is used in most dishes, both cooked and uncooked. It is ground to a medium-fine grain so that it still retains a little texture. The exception in its use is any dish which contains fresh chili. The fresh sweetness of the hot chili gives such a different flavour to a dish that black and white peppercorns would be completely out of place.

CHILI

We buy our red, green and yellow chilies from all over the world and each delivery seems to have different levels of hotness and sweetness. It is therefore necessary while cooking with them to experiment, adding a small amount at a time until the required amount of spiciness is achieved. We chop the whole chili, including the seeds but excluding the stem, very finely before adding it to a dish. When they are used as a seasoning ingredient in long-cooked dishes such as soups which will eventually be puréed they can be added either whole or simply cut in half. It is important to note that fingers stained with the juice of chili must never be placed near the eyes as it can result in a very painful stinging sensation.

OLIVE OIL

Every day in Clarke's kitchen we use up to five different olive oils, produced in Tuscany, Umbria, Spain and Sicily. During an average year we use well over three thousand litres. The oils range from a simple extra virgin, which is used in the basic preparations of our cooking, to a very extravagant first cold pressing olive oil which we use simply for drizzling over a finished dish or simple salad.

In the following recipes I have suggested the use of just two types: an inexpensive one which can be used for cooking and a finer, deeper coloured, fully flavoured one for finished dishes, salads and pasta. These tend to be much more expensive but are well worth the extravagance. They are described in the recipes as olive oil and good olive oil.

VINEGARS

One of my next projects will be to create our own vinegar at the restaurant. Once I find a 'vinegar mother', leftover drops of wine from bottles on the tables could be added to the barrel and allowed to ferment, thus creating our own style of vinegar. However, in the meanwhile we use two commercially made vinegars in our kitchen, *aceto balsamico* (balsamic vinegar) and champagne wine vinegar. The expensive balsamic vinegar is made in the area around Modena in Italy and involves a long process in which the wine is first boiled to create a rich, slightly sweetened liquid, then over a period of many years it is transferred from one type of wooden barrel to another (the more variety of woods used, the more complex the eventual flavours will be) as it matures, sweetens and deepens in colour.

We do not make 'salad dressings' as such in the restaurant. If the leaves, vegetables or fruits are perfect and the olive oil fruity and rich, the addition of flaked Maldon salt, a crack of pepper and perhaps a little freshly chopped herb is sufficient to embellish them. On the rare occasions when vinegar is used in a salad, we use approximately one part balsamic vinegar to three parts olive oil.

Champagne wine vinegar is used in dishes which do not require the sweet-ness, richness or expense of a balsamic. If a sharper more acidic flavour is needed, or if many other ingredients are being used, this vinegar is perfect, such as in mustard sauces, pickling or chutney making. I would not use it in a simple salad as it would be too sharp and acidic and would speed the wilting process of the leaves. As an alternative a little squeeze of lemon or lime juice is a perfect addition.

GAME STOCK

To make approximately 1 litre

1 kg venison bones
3 chicken carcasses, approximately 1.5kg, trimmed of excess fat and parson's noses
2 large onions, peeled and cut in half
6 outside stalks of celery, washed and chopped
3 large carrots peeled, trimmed and cut in half lengthwise
1 large leek, outer leaves removed, cut into half lengthwise, washed well
1 large fennel, washed and cut into quarters
sprigs of bay, rosemary, thyme and sage
1 head garlic, cut in half across the circumference, decaying cloves removed
1 tsp mixed black and white peppercorns
½ bottle good hearty red wine

FOR THE REDUCTION
25g unsalted butter
1 onion, peeled and cut into fine dice
1 large carrot, peeled, washed and chopped fine
2 stalks celery, washed and chopped fine
3 cloves garlic, crushed whole
½ bottle good hearty red wine
sprigs of thyme, rosemary, sage and Italian flat-leaf parsley

Preheat the oven to 180°C/350°F/gas mark 4.

Ask your butcher to chop the bones for you so that they are not overlarge. Place them in a roasting tin and roast for 20–25 minutes or until rich dark brown. Take care when checking the bones as the natural darkness of their colour can be deceptive. On no account should they cook for too long as they can easily burn. Place the chicken carcasses in a separate roasting tin and roast until dark golden.

Place the vegetables in a tall stock pot and add all the bones. Add the herbs, garlic, peppercorns, red wine and water to cover and bring to the boil. Skim well, turn the heat down, move the pan to half cover the heat and simmer for

8 hours, skimming when necessary. The level of the stock should not noticeably reduce but as it simmers it will increase in clarity and depth of colour. Strain through a fine strainer and cool as rapidly as possible over a bowl of ice. Refrigerate overnight and skim away the fat from the surface, then reduce by a third, as follows.

For the reduction

In a heavy-based pan heat the butter until the foam subsides, add the vegetables and stir occasionally until golden brown. Pour in the red wine and herbs and reduce by half. Pour the stock in carefully, leaving any sediment behind. Bring to the boil, skim and then place on half the heat source to reduce by a third, skimming whenever necessary. It should appear glossy, dark and richly coloured. Strain through a fine strainer and cool over a bowl of ice. This will keep refrigerated for up to 5 days in a sealed container or for 6 months in the freezer.

SEASONAL MENUS

In the pages which follow each season has an example of a lunch, supper and dinner menu with an '&' section displaying an extended range of restaurant and home dishes which can be interwoven into the menus depending on taste or the style of the occasion.

Generally the lunches are simple to serve and not too time consuming in the preparation, thus allowing the cook to be free to enjoy the meal and be free to entertain guests also.

Supper to me means an informal or light meal which can also be served with the minimum amount of to-ing and fro-ing to the kitchen. The dishes chosen for these menus tend to need a certain amount of preparation time but once they have been assembled, the serving is relatively uncomplicated.

The dinners probably reflect Clarke's restaurant menus more than the others, involving a little more skill in preparation, patience and good timing. However, none of the dishes is overly fussy or unnecessarily complicated. None of our cooking is. It is simple, pure and, I hope, unpretentious. It allows the ingredients to speak and shine for themselves. The presentation of your dishes should reflect that too.

The many dishes suitable for vegetarians and vegans are marked † and ‡ respectively in the index.

ALL RECIPES ARE FOR 6 SERVINGS
UNLESS OTHERWISE STATED.

SPRING

LUNCH

Parsley Soup with Morel Mushrooms
& Crème Fraiche

Pissaladière

Grilled Spring Asparagus with
Parmesan & Balsamic Dressing

Salad of Spring Vegetables
with San Daniele Ham, Quails' Eggs
& Roasted Garlic Mayonnaise

Marinated Olives

Lemon Curd Cream Puff
with Candied Lemon

LUNCH PICNIC ON A TABLE

There is nothing more appetizing than a table laid with a tempting array of dishes of varying temperatures that can be served in a comfortable informal way, allowing guests to help themselves to as little or as much as they wish and at the pace that they wish. It has obvious advantages if the dietary preferences of the guests are unknown. Vegetarians and fish eaters as well as carnivores can be made to feel equally at home with a selection of dishes in front of them. The advantages are obvious also to the cook, as so much can be prepared in advance and assembled as guests sit down. It is important, however, that the dishes appear fresh. A salad tossed at the last minute looks bright and vibrant whereas a salad tossed too far in advance, wilting in the acidity of the dressing, is sad, unappealing and a waste.

For these reasons I have suggested a menu which can be eaten as a 'picnic' but one which is actually served indoors at a table with all the advantages of heating or cooling facilities at hand and a washing-up sink nearby. On a perfect spring day this could be arranged at the kitchen table with the back door open, allowing the feeling of fresh air and sunlight to pour in, but equally this could be designed to be more formal if there is a dining room away from the preparation area.

PARSLEY SOUP WITH MOREL MUSHROOMS & CRÈME FRAICHE

60ml olive oil

75g unsalted butter

*300g potatoes (preferably King Edward or Maris Piper),
    peeled and cut into walnut-sized pieces*

5 stalks celery, chopped roughly

2 medium leeks, trimmed, cut in half and sliced roughly

2 small heads fennel, trimmed and sliced roughly

*400g picked Italian flat-leaf parsley leaves (approximately 3 generous bunches),
    and their stalks*

salt and pepper

250g spinach leaves, stalks removed, washed gently but thoroughly

TO SERVE

3 tbsp olive oil

*300g morel mushrooms or a selection of wild mushrooms, brushed and broken into
    even-sized pieces (if wild mushrooms are not available, use black flat field
    mushrooms peeled and cut into cubes)*

1 tsp chopped thyme leaves

1 tbsp roughly chopped Italian flat-leaf parsley leaves

90ml crème fraiche

6 small sprigs of Italian flat-leaf parsley

Warm the olive oil gently with the butter in a heavy-based pan and add the potato, celery, leeks and fennel. Cook over a gentle heat, stirring occasionally. The vegetables should not be allowed to colour, instead they should gently soften whilst absorbing the oil and butter. Add the parsley stalks, salt, pepper and enough water to cover. Bring to the boil, cover and simmer for 20–25 minutes or until the vegetables are soft. Add all but a few of the parsley leaves with the spinach leaves and bring back to the boil, stirring continuously for 2–3 minutes whilst the leaves wilt.

Place the solids from the pan into a liquidizer or food processor and purée, gradually adding a little of the liquid until a creamy consistency is reached. (It may not be necessary to use all the liquid – alternatively, a little extra water may be needed.)

Pass the soup through a medium-fine sieve into a metal container, pushing the solids through as hard as possible with the back of a ladle or spoon. Place the base of the container into a bowl of ice and pour enough cold water over the ice to come halfway up the side. Stir the soup occasionally whilst it chills. This immediate chilling will help retain the bright green colour. Taste and adjust the seasoning if necessary.

To serve, warm 6 soup plates.

In a heavy-based frying pan, heat the olive oil and add the mushrooms and thyme, tossing gently, then the remaining parsley leaves and season with salt and pepper. Leave on one side. Reheat the soup gently, without boiling, and pour the soup into the plates. Place the mushrooms in the centre of each plate and garnish with a generous scoop of crème fraiche and a sprig of parsley.

PISSALADIÈRE

If asked to choose a handful of dishes that typified Provence, I am sure that most people would choose Pissaladière as one of them. It is traditionally baked using leftover bread dough, roasted onions, salty olives and anchovy fillets; an ideal snack food, or, as in this menu, an accompaniment to other foods as an alternative to bread.

To serve 6–8 as a first course or 10–12 as a part of a 'picnic' menu

FOR THE FOCACCIA DOUGH
200g flour
5g salt
10g fresh yeast or 5g dried yeast
100ml warm water
60ml olive oil

FOR THE FILLING
4 large onions, peeled, halved and sliced finely
75ml olive oil
2 tsp roughly chopped thyme leaves
Maldon salt and pepper
12 fillets of salted anchovies, rinsed and patted dry, or anchovies in oil, drained
24 soft marinated black olives, pitted (do not even dream of using the tinned pitted
   'olives' in brine)

TO FINISH
a handful of parsley leaves
good olive oil

Sieve the flour into a bowl with the salt. Mix the yeast with the water until smooth and pour into the flour, incorporating the flour gradually. Finally add the olive oil until a soft and slightly sticky dough is formed. Turn the dough out on to a lightly floured table and knead gently until smooth and springy to the touch when prodded with a finger. This may take up to 10 minutes. Alternatively, use a mixing machine on the lowest speed with the dough-hook attachment, mixing for approximately 5–7 minutes.

Smear a little olive oil over the inside of a medium-sized bowl, place the dough inside, cover with cling film and leave in a draught-free warm place until the dough has doubled in bulk, approximately 45 minutes.

Meanwhile prepare the filling ingredients. Place the onions in a heavy-based pan with the olive oil and cook over a high heat until they have turned golden brown. Add the thyme, salt and pepper and pour into a bowl to cool.

On a lightly floured surface, roll out the focaccia dough into a disc approximately 18 cm across. Lightly brush the surface of a heavy baking sheet with olive oil and place the dough on top.

Spread the onions evenly over the surface, leaving an outside rim of 2cm uncovered. Cover with cling film and leave in a warm place to prove for 10–15 minutes whilst preheating the oven to 180°C/350°F/gas mark 4. Bake for 15 minutes or until the crust has begun to puff. Remove from the oven and place the anchovies and olives on the top decoratively. Continue to bake for a further 5 minutes or until the crust is golden. Serve cool or immediately, sprinkled with a few parsley leaves and drizzled with a little olive oil.

GRILLED SPRING ASPARAGUS WITH PARMESAN & BALSAMIC DRESSING

FOR THE BALSAMIC DRESSING
90 ml olive oil
30 ml balsamic vinegar
Maldon salt and pepper
1 tbsp chopped chives

FOR THE ASPARAGUS
800g thin green asparagus, the width of two pencils if available
olive oil for grilling
Maldon salt and pepper
150g piece of Parmesan, grated on the fine side of the grater

TO GARNISH
1 small bunch of chives, cut into 4 cm lengths

Mix all the dressing ingredients together well and taste. Adjust for seasoning.

Heat the char grill to its highest heat or warm a griddle pan gently then brush with a little olive oil (see page 170 for char-grilling notes).

Trim the asparagus of the tough ends and wash. If they are fat, they may need a gentle peeling with a potato peeler at the base end.

Using fine metal or wooden skewers, skewer together 5 or 6 asparagus per person, keeping them straight. Trim the excess ends off with a sharp knife to make the lengths even. Pile the skewers on to a plate and just before grilling drizzle the asparagus with olive oil and season with salt and pepper. Turn them over gently and rub the other side in the excess oil.

Place on the grill at a criss-cross angle and grill for a minute or two or until bar marks appear. Turn over and grill again for a few seconds or until they become tender. Remove to a plate and carefully pull out the skewers. Arrange the asparagus on individual serving dishes. Sprinkle with Maldon salt, place the grated Parmesan on top, then a grinding or two of black pepper, and finally pour a fine drizzle of the balsamic dressing over the plate. Garnish with the chives and serve.

SALAD OF SPRING VEGETABLES WITH SAN DANIELE HAM, QUAILS' EGGS & ROASTED GARLIC MAYONNAISE

This hors d'oeuvres platter may display a selection of any vegetables which look fresh and healthy. The list given below is only for guidance, but it is important to bear in mind colours and shapes when choosing your selection.

FOR THE ROASTED GARLIC MAYONNAISE

3 cloves garlic, preferably new season 'pink', peeled and cut in half,
    green shoot removed if present
250ml olive oil
1 organic or free range egg
1 organic or free range egg yolk
juice of ½ lemon
salt and pepper

FOR THE SALAD

2 bay leaves
a handful of small young carrots, with tops trimmed to 1cm, rinsed well
6 small globe artichokes, the tips of the leaves and most of the stems trimmed away
18 quails' eggs
12–18 slices of San Daniele ham or prosciutto, depending on size
6 young fennel bulbs, trimmed, or 2 large bulbs, cut into wedges
12 spring onions, trimmed of root and top and rinsed
heart of 1 celery, stalks trimmed to even lengths, leaves attached
2 Belgian endive cut in sixths, core removed
Maldon salt and pepper
good olive oil
2 bunches of radishes (approximately 30), trimmed of any wilting leaves
    and washed well

Place the garlic in a tiny pan and drizzle with 1–2 tbsp olive oil. Place over a low heat and pan-roast very gently until soft and golden. Allow to cool in the oil.

Whisk the egg and egg yolk together in a bowl and slowly add the remaining oil drop by drop until it begins to thicken. At this stage the oil can be added a little faster, with the addition of a drop of lemon juice from time to time. Gently crush the garlic with its oil and fold this in, with salt and pepper to taste. Spoon into a serving pot.

Bring a stainless-steel pan of salted water to the boil, add the bay leaves and cook the carrots for a minute or two or just long enough for them to lose their natural crispness. Remove to a plate with a slotted spoon and allow to cool. In the same pan cook the artichokes completely submerged in the water by covering them with a small pan lid. When a wooden skewer passes through the stem easily, drain and rinse under cold water. Peel the tough outer leaves away and cut the artichoke in half, removing the choke if present.

Place the quails' eggs in a pan of cold water, slowly bring them to the boil and then immediately cool them under running cold water. Do not peel, as I believe that the shell is far prettier than the peeled egg.

Choose a large serving platter and arrange the slices of ham over half the dish in gentle folds. Place the pot of mayonnaise in the centre of the dish. Put all the vegetables except the radishes in a large bowl. Toss gently with the salt, pepper and olive oil and arrange attractively on the second half of the dish. Add the radishes and the eggs and serve.

MARINATED OLIVES

At the restaurant we use a variety of olives in as many ways. The green and black olives we buy from Provence are marinated in extra-virgin olive oil and herbes de Provence for months before canning and as a result are soft, juicy and full of flavour. The tiny pointed picholine olives from France are delivered in jars in a salty brine, as are my favourites, the tiny black-purple Niçoise olives. These types of olives are expensive and not easy to find but there is no point whatsoever in cutting costs for this recipe. The rubbery acidic black and green 'cocktail' olives found in most corner shops are *not* to be used here.

approximately 600g of as many different good quality olives as affordable
peelings from 1 lemon and 1 orange, taken off with either a vegetable peeler
    or a sharp knife
1 small bunch of thyme, sprigs picked to equal lengths
8 fresh bay leaves
1 small chili, sliced in half lengthwise, with stalk attached
1 clove garlic, peeled and sliced into fine slivers
60ml olive oil

Mix the ingredients well together and leave to marinate for at least 1 hour. Serve in a dish with the bay leaves, thyme and chili acting as their garnish.

LEMON CURD CREAM PUFF
WITH CANDIED LEMON

FOR THE CHOUX PASTRY
100g flour
a pinch of salt
a pinch of sugar
185ml water
85g butter
3 eggs, beaten

FOR THE LEMON CURD
(This amount will make more than the recipe requires but it is perfect for teatime,
*   spread on fresh bread or freshly baked scones)*
finely grated zest and juice of 2 lemons
125g sugar
5 egg yolks
175g unsalted butter, at room temperature

FOR THE CARAMELIZED LEMON PEEL
2 lemons, peeled using a vegetable peeler (approximately 12 peelings)
150g sugar
250ml water

TO ASSEMBLE
200ml double cream, whipped to stiff peaks
6 sprigs of mint and icing sugar for decoration

For the choux pastry

Sieve the flour, salt and sugar together twice. In a heavy-based pan heat the water and butter together gently until the butter has melted. Bring to a rolling boil and add the flour immediately, stirring well until smooth. Take off the heat and gradually beat in the eggs until a glossy soft paste is achieved.

Preheat the oven to 180°C/350°F/gas mark 4. Brush a heavy metal baking sheet with a little extra melted butter.

Using a tablespoon place the choux mixture on the tray, allowing generous spaces between each one, and bake for 10–15 minutes or until puffed and golden. Turn the oven temperature down to 150°C/300°F/gas mark 2 and continue to cook until dry on the inside, approximately 15–20 minutes. Remove from the baking sheet to a cooling rack. With a small knife make a small incision in the side of each bun to release the steam. Allow to cool.

For the lemon curd

In a medium-sized bowl mix the lemon zest, juice, sugar and egg yolks together until well blended. Place the bowl over a pan of gently steaming water on a low heat, and stir continuously with a scrupulously clean wooden spoon as the curd warms and begins to thicken. When it starts to coat the back of the spoon, approximately 6–8 minutes, remove the bowl from the pan and gently stir in the butter until melted. Strain through a stainless-steel or plastic strainer into a clean bowl and allow to cool. It will keep for 7 days in a refrigerator.

For the caramelized lemon peel

Place all the ingredients in a small heavy-based pan and warm them gently until the sugar melts. Turn up the heat and simmer gently until the volume is reduced by three-quarters. The thick syrup will be a deep lemon colour. Pour into a bowl and cool.

To assemble

Split the choux buns in half horizontally and scoop out any uncooked dough from the inside. Mix the whipped cream with half the lemon curd and fold together gently. Spoon the cream into the bases of the buns and cover with the tops. Arrange on serving dishes, and decorate with the lemon peelings, a little of the syrup and a mint sprig dusted with icing sugar.

SUPPER

Hazelnut & Raisin Bread

Goat's Cheese & Thyme Soufflé

Slow-Baked Duck Leg with Onion 'Marmalade',
Duck-Fat Roasted Potatoes & Bitter Leaf Salad

Pink Grapefruit & Vin d'Orange Sorbet;
Honey Madeleines

HAZELNUT & RAISIN BREAD

400g strong white flour
100g rye flour
10g salt
15g yeast
300ml warm water
180g shelled hazelnuts
100g raisins

In a mixing bowl mix the flours well with the salt. In a small bowl mix the yeast with half the water and using the dough-hook attachment on the slowest speed gently mix the liquids into the flour, adding the remaining warm water as necessary to produce a soft dough. Continue to mix for 5–6 minutes or until the dough is smooth and shiny. Add the hazelnuts and raisins and mix thoroughly. Alternatively the mixing can be done by hand in a medium-sized bowl and then turned out on to a clean table and kneaded for 5–10 minutes until smooth.

Place the dough in a clean bowl, cover with cling film and leave in a warm place until it has almost doubled in bulk, approximately 1 hour.

Preheat the oven to 180°C/350°F/gas mark 4. Turn the dough out on to a lightly floured surface and knead again to expel any excess air. Cut into two and roll into two balls. Dust a baking sheet with a little white flour and lay the breads side by side, allowing room for growth as they prove again. Cover with cling film and leave in a warm place to rise at least half again in size.

Place on the middle shelf of the oven, immediately raise the temperature to 190°C/375°F/gas mark 5 and bake for 30–35 minutes or until the crusts are pale golden and the bases sound hollow when knocked. Cool and eat within 2 days.

GOAT'S CHEESE & THYME SOUFFLÉ

One of the first dishes I ever tasted at Chez Panisse in California was a cheese soufflé. It was not baked in a traditional soufflé dish nor did it have the appearance of a traditional soufflé. Instead, Alice had cooked it on a flat ovenproof plate which was brought to the table from which to serve oneself. It looked so unusual that I was keen to experiment with the idea in my own kitchen the following day. I do not know Alice's recipe, but this is a recipe which we cooked when presenting a vegetarian menu to a customer some years ago. It is quick and simple, does not require a prolonged cooking time and does not involve the preparation of the usual roux base.

30g unsalted butter, melted
200g freshly grated Parmesan
6 fresh free-range eggs
400g fresh soft goat's cheese
150ml double cream
1 tsp chopped thyme
salt and pepper
a few thyme leaves

Preheat the oven to 200°C/400°F/gas mark 6.

Butter 6 ovenproof soup plates (preferably flat – not bowls) and sprinkle with a quarter of the Parmesan.

Whisk the egg yolks until smooth, add the goat's cheese and whisk again. Stir in the cream and season with the chopped thyme and salt and pepper. Fold in half of the remaining Parmesan. In a separate clean dry bowl whisk the whites with a pinch of salt until stiff peaks are formed. Fold the whites carefully but thoroughly into the cheese mixture, divide between the dishes and sprinkle with the thyme leaves and remaining Parmesan. Place on a baking sheet in the oven and bake until risen and golden, approximately 8–10 minutes. Serve immediately, remembering to warn guests that the dishes are oven hot!

SLOW-BAKED DUCK LEG WITH ONION 'MARMALADE', DUCK-FAT ROASTED POTATOES & BITTER-LEAF SALAD

Confit is the classic way of preserving duck in the south-west of France and this slow baking method results in a meltingly tender flesh enriched in flavour by the infused garlic and herbs. It is perfect to eat in the colder months, late autumn to early spring, as it is such a comforting dish. Summer holiday time in the Dordogne is *not* the season to taste the slow-baked local duck and goose confits, even though it seems every restaurant there advertises this speciality all year round.

To prepare the confit

FOR THE MARINADE
30g Maldon salt
10g crushed black peppercorns
½ small bunch of thyme, roughly chopped
½ small bunch of rosemary, roughly chopped
6 bay leaves, roughly chopped
1 whole head garlic, roughly chopped
3 tbsp cognac
6 duck legs

FOR THE DUCK
1.5kg duck fat or goose fat
4 cloves garlic, crushed
½ bunch of thyme
3 bay leaves

Mix together the salt, peppercorns, herbs, garlic, and cognac, and scatter half over the base of a dish wide enough to hold the duck legs. Place the legs tightly together, fat side down and side by side, and scatter the remaining salt mixture

over the top. Cover closely with a piece of cling film, then a dish which fits snugly on top of the duck. Stand a heavy weight such as a bag of flour on top to press the marinating ingredients into the duck. Place in the refrigerator and leave to marinate for 2 days, then remove the dish from the refrigerator and discard any liquid which may have drained from the duck. Turn the pieces of duck over, cover and press as before and return to the refrigerator for 2 more days then scrape all the marinade from the duck and dry the legs with a paper towel.

Gently heat the duck or goose fat with the garlic and herbs in a heavy-based pan. Add the legs and bring to a simmer. On a very low heat cook the legs for 2–2½ hours or until a metal skewer moves easily through the meat. Allow the duck legs to cool in the fat and when cool enough to handle remove them and trim away the knuckle and any excess fat from the sides of the leg. Place them into a scrupulously clean pot or dish, heat the fat to boiling point and strain it over them to cover them completely. Discard the garlic and herb debris. Allow to cool and then keep refrigerated until required.

ONION 'MARMALADE'

Makes 6 small jars

1.5kg onions, peeled and sliced as finely as possible
2 tbsp salt
1.2kg sugar
600ml champagne vinegar or white wine vinegar
1 tsp cloves wrapped in a muslin bag
2½ tsp caraway seeds

Place the onions in a bowl with the salt. Cover and leave for a minimum of 1 hour in a cool place or refrigerator. Rinse and drain. Simmer the sugar with the vinegar and cloves for 5 minutes. Add the onion and caraway seeds, return to the boil and simmer carefully for 2–2½ hours. Meanwhile preheat the oven to 180°C/350°F/gas mark 4. Lay the scrupulously clean jam jars on a baking sheet and sterilize in the oven for 10 minutes. Boil the lids in a small pan of water for 5 minutes to sterilize. When the syrup is thick and the onions are translucent, pour it into the jars.

This will keep in a very cool place or refrigerator for up to 1 month.

SLOW-BAKED DUCK LEG & DUCK-FAT ROASTED POTATOES

3 large potatoes (preferably Desirée), washed and cut in halves or quarters, depending on the size
Maldon salt
approximately 75g duck fat
pepper
1 small bunch of thyme, leaves only
6 confited duck legs

Preheat the oven to 180°C/350°F/gas mark 4.

With a small sharp knife make a few criss-cross marks through the cut surface of the potato approximately halfway through to the skin. Bring the potatoes to the boil in salted water and simmer for 5–8 minutes or until half cooked. Drain well and place in a roasting pan, cut side up, with three-quarters of the duck fat and sprinkle with salt, pepper and half the thyme. Roast for approximately 30–35 minutes or until golden, basting occasionally and checking that they do not stick to the pan.

Meanwhile, carefully remove the legs from the fat and place them skin-side down in a heavy-based ovenproof frying pan with the remaining fat. Warm them gently until the fat melts and roast them in the oven for 15 minutes or until crisp. Remove from the oven, turn them over and return them to the oven for 5 more minutes. Alternatively, place them in the roasting pan with the potatoes in the last 15–20 minutes of their cooking. Sprinkle the duck and potatoes with the remaining thyme, remove to a serving platter and serve with onion marmalade and bitter leaf salad.

BITTER LEAF SALAD

Ideally a salad should be made with ingredients freshly picked from the garden, or chosen directly from the market stall. At Clarke's we are lucky to have access to gardeners in the south-east who grow and pick salad ingredients specially for us and then deliver them daily to our door. Obviously not everyone has this luxury and many have to rely on local shops to provide the vitamin C element of their menus. Although most supermarkets now offer a range of mixed salad leaves, bagged in plastic, too often they appear sweaty or wilting and not at their best.

If only we all had a farmers' market in our town. In village markets across the Channel the boxes of various bitter leaves are brought from the surrounding areas, often by the growers themselves. Shoppers there have the choice of young spinach leaves, landcress, watercress, dandelion leaves, red and white chicory, trevisse, white tinged with red, and red tinged with white, rocket of all lengths, shapes and degrees of pepperiness, sorrel, corn salad (mâche or lamb's lettuce), and herbs such as chervil, parsley, coriander and salad burnet.

The ingredients listed below are only for guidance. If a greater selection of leaves is available to you, choose as many types as you wish.

1 head radicchio or trevisse
1 head Belgian endive, red or white
1 bunch of watercress
1 bunch of landcress if available, or rocket, long stalks removed
1 bunch of dandelion leaves, long stalks removed
a few small sprigs of Italian flat-leaf parsley
Maldon salt and pepper
approximately 6 tsp good olive oil
1 tbsp chives chopped 2 cm long

Trim the base away from the radicchio and Belgian endive and gently separate the leaves. Pick sprigs from each stem of the watercress. Place all the salad leaves in a bowl of cold water and leave to rinse for a few minutes. Drain the leaves gently and spin in a salad spinner, place in a large bowl, and sprinkle with salt, pepper and olive oil. Toss carefully, scatter with chives and serve.

PINK GRAPEFRUIT & VIN D'ORANGE SORBET; HONEY MADELEINES

In the absence of vin d'orange, a good sweet wine may be used instead (a Beaumes de Venise would be ideal).

100ml water
200g sugar
1 vanilla pod, split in two lengthwise
600ml pink grapefruit juice
150ml Vin d'Orange (page 88), or sweet white wine

Bring the water to the boil in a heavy-based saucepan with the sugar and vanilla pod and simmer for 5 minutes. Mix the grapefruit juice, wine and syrup together. Churn the sorbet in an ice-cream machine according to the manufacturer's instructions and store in a deep freeze. Alternatively make a granita by pouring the liquid into an ice-making tray and placing it in the freezer. Remove the tray from the freezer every 15–20 minutes and scratch the ice crystals with a fork until it has frozen; depending on the efficiency of your freezer this may take up to 2 hours. Breaking up the ice crystals will prevent the granita forming one solid lump of ice as it freezes.

This sorbet or granita will keep well for 24 hours but will lose its flavour and consistency if kept for longer. Serve in tall glasses on plates covered with paper doilies accompanied by Honey Madeleines.

HONEY MADELEINES

Ideally the baking tins made specifically for madeleines should be used, but in their absence use cocktail-size paper cups or other small muffin moulds.

110g plain flour
2 eggs
50g sugar
50g honey, plus 2 tbsp gently warmed for brushing on after cooking
90g butter, melted and cooled
finely grated zest of 1 lemon
soft butter and flour for brushing the madeleine moulds

Sieve the flour twice. Whisk the eggs with the sugar and the 50g honey until light and fluffy. Fold in the flour gently, followed by the butter and lemon zest. Allow to rest in a refrigerator for up to 1 hour.

Preheat the oven to 180°C/350°F/gas mark 4. Brush the madeleine moulds thoroughly with a little soft butter and dust with flour. Spoon the mixture into the moulds and bake for 8–10 minutes or until puffed and golden. Remove from the moulds, brush with the gently warmed honey and cool on a rack.

DINNER

CORNMEAL ROLLS

SALAD OF BLACK TRUFFLE, WATERCRESS,
PINK FIR APPLE POTATO CRISPS
& CRÈME FRAICHE

GRILLED SKEWERED SCALLOPS WITH GREMOLATA,
SPROUTING BROCCOLI & SEA KALE

WIGMORE CHEESE WITH OATMEAL BISCUITS

SOFT PISTACHIO MERINGUE WITH
BLOOD ORANGES & RHUBARB

CORNMEAL ROLLS

100g medium ground cornmeal (not cornflour), plus a small amount for sprinkling
250ml boiling water
400g strong white flour
10g salt
10g fresh yeast or 5g dried yeast
5g sugar
50ml milk
approximately 50ml warm water
a little extra cornmeal and flour for dusting

Sprinkle the cornmeal into the boiling water in a small pan and beat over a low heat with a wooden spoon until thick and smooth, approximately 3 minutes. Leave to cool.

Mix the cooled cornmeal, flour and salt together well in a mixing bowl. In a small bowl mix the yeast with the sugar and milk and half the warm water until the yeast has become liquid. Using the slowest speed and the dough-hook attachment of a mixing machine, slowly pour the liquid into the flour, adding almost all the remaining warm water until a soft dough is formed and all the flour has been gathered together. Continue to mix until the dough looks smooth and shiny, approximately 5–8 minutes. Alternatively the mixing can be done by hand in a medium-sized bowl and then turned out on to a clean table and kneaded for 5–10 minutes until smooth.

Place the dough in a clean bowl, cover with cling film and allow to rise in a warm, not hot, place until almost doubled in bulk. This may take up to 1 hour depending on the temperature of the kitchen and the weather. Preheat the oven to 180°C/350°F/gas mark 4 and sprinkle the baking sheet with a little cornmeal. Turn the dough out on to a clean table dusted with a small amount of flour and knead again to expel all the air.

Cut into 12 equal-sized pieces and shape into balls. Place them on the baking sheet allowing space in between each one. Dust with a little flour, cover with cling film and allow them to rise to half their size again in a warm place. This may take up to 30 minutes. Place the tray on the middle rack in the oven, and immediately turn up the heat to 205°C/400°F/gas mark 6 and bake for 20–25 minutes or until golden brown. This raising of the temperature will assist in the 'lift' of the dough in the initial cooking stages. Cool and serve within a day.

SALAD OF BLACK TRUFFLE, WATERCRESS, PINK FIR APPLE POTATO CRISPS & CRÈME FRAICHE

Pink fir apple potatoes, known predominantly for their use in salads because of their sweetness and waxy texture, fry beautifully if sliced thinly and eaten immediately. If they are difficult to find, use another frying potato instead. Although I like the combination of the 'prince and the pauper' being presented together on the same plate, if the truffle proves to be impossibly expensive, this salad will still be more than acceptable without it.

1 small black truffle, approximately 30g
2 tbsp chives chopped small
Maldon salt and pepper
1 tbsp balsamic vinegar
3 tbsp good olive oil
2 bunches of watercress
500g pink fir apple or Desirée potatoes
vegetable oil for frying
90ml crème fraiche

Brush the truffle to remove any sand from the crevices. Slice off a quarter from one side and chop this very finely. Place the chopped truffle in a bowl with the chives, salt, pepper, balsamic vinegar and olive oil. Leave on one side to infuse. Wrap the remaining piece of truffle well until required for shaving over the finished salad. Pick the watercress into sprigs, rinse in cold water and spin in a salad spinner. Place in a bowl and keep cool. Wash then slice the potatoes finely with a very sharp knife or mandolin. Place in a colander under running cold water and rinse for a few seconds to release the excess starch. Spin the potato slices in a salad spinner until dry or drain thoroughly on kitchen paper.

To serve, heat the vegetable oil to 180°C/350°F. Fry a small amount at a time until crisp and golden. Drain well on kitchen paper, sprinkle with salt and keep warm. Toss the watercress with the black truffle dressing, arrange on serving plates layered with the crisps and shave the truffle over immediately. Place a dessertspoonful of crème fraiche on the top of each salad and serve.

GRILLED SKEWERED SCALLOPS WITH GREMOLATA, SPROUTING BROCCOLI & SEA KALE

18 large scallops, trimmed of the muscle and rinsed gently
black pepper
olive oil

GREMOLATA
leaves of 1 large bunch of Italian flat-leaf parsley, roughly chopped
grated zest of 1 lemon
½ tsp Maldon salt
1 green chili, chopped very fine
1 shallot, diced very fine

TO SERVE
500g sprouting broccoli
750g sea kale
good olive oil
6 lemon wedges, pips removed

Heat the grill to its highest setting at least 10 minutes before cooking, or heat a griddle pan gently with a little vegetable oil.

Holding 2 skewers approximately 2cm apart, thread 3 scallops together making sure that each roe is neatly positioned between each one. Continue with

the remaining skewers and scallops. Lay them on a plate and sprinkle with pepper and drizzle with a little olive oil.

Mix the gremolata ingredients together.

Trim the thick stem away from the broccoli, releasing the small florets at the base of the stem. Continue to cut away more of the base, releasing more of the florets until each head is left with a few leaves surrounding it.

Wash the broccoli florets.

Trim the sea kale by removing the base, leaving the small heart whole, and trimming the stalks to even lengths. Wash gently but thoroughly.

Grill the skewers at a slight angle to the bars, criss-cross after a minute and grill again until well seared. Turn and cook again until seared. Depending on the heat of the grill and the thickness of the scallop, this may take up to 3–5 minutes, but take care as scallops can easily be overcooked. They should feel firm to the touch but should be juicy and tender on the inside.

Meanwhile bring two pans of salted water to the boil and cook the two vegetables separately (they will take slightly different lengths of time to cook), until al dente, approximately 2–3 minutes. Drain and place in a bowl, drizzle with olive oil, salt and pepper, toss together and arrange with the grilled scallops with a spoonful of gremolata over the top, a drizzle of good olive oil and the lemon wedges.

OATMEAL BISCUITS

Makes 24 biscuits

250g medium-ground oatmeal
125g flour
125g wholemeal flour
½ tsp bicarbonate of soda
1 tsp salt
1 tsp caster sugar
250g butter, cold
1 egg, beaten

Mix all the dry ingredients together and rub in the butter until it resembles bread-crumbs. Add the egg and form a soft dough. Preheat the oven to 180°C/350°F/gas mark 4. Chill the dough for 30 minutes before rolling into a thin sheet. Cut with a 5cm fluted biscuit cutter, lay on a baking sheet and bake for 8–10 minutes. The biscuits will become crisp on cooling.

SOFT PISTACHIO MERINGUE WITH BLOOD ORANGES & RHUBARB

3 egg whites

190g sugar

2 tsp cornflour

1 tsp champagne wine vinegar

½ tsp vanilla essence

50g shelled unsalted pistachio nuts, roughly chopped

200g forced rhubarb (approximately 3 sticks)

50g sugar

75ml blood orange juice

75ml inexpensive sweet white wine, e.g. Jurançon or Beaumes de Venise

250ml double cream, whipped to soft peaks

6 large blood oranges, peeled of peel and pith, cut into segments

6 sprigs of mint

Preheat the oven to 140°C/285°F/gas mark 1 and line a baking sheet with silicone wax paper.

In a clean dry bowl whisk the egg whites until stiff then fold in the sugar gradually, whisking continually until the meringue becomes thick and glossy. Finally whisk in the cornflour, vinegar and vanilla essence. Fold in the pistachio nuts.

Scoop the meringue into 6 equal-sized mounds on the baking sheet, leaving a small space between each one as they will puff a little during cooking.

Bake for approximately 40 minutes or until crisp on the outside but not coloured. The interior should be soft and marshmallow-like.

Meanwhile prepare the rhubarb. Cut it into lengths of 4–5cm and place these in an ovenproof dish. Sprinkle with the sugar, orange juice and wine, cover with aluminium foil and bake in the same oven for 10–15 minutes or until tender. Allow to cool. Choose and reserve the most beautiful 18 pieces of rhubarb and

push the remaining pieces through a plastic sieve with all the cooking juices. Taste for sweetness.

To assemble, place 6 meringues on 6 plates, top each one with a spoonful of whipped cream and arrange the orange segments and reserved rhubarb attractively. Serve immediately with the rhubarb sauce drizzled over and a mint sprig.

& SPRING

Vin d'Orange

Salad of Globe Artichokes & Pink Grapefruit
with Black Olive Dressing

Potato & Chive Frittata

Sweet-Sour Onions

Ravioli of Ricotta, Goat's Cheese & Parmesan
with Sage & Artichokes

Fish Cakes with Tartare Sauce

Warm Smoked Eel with Crisp Pancetta,
Trevisse & Dill Soured Cream

Marinated Fresh Anchovies

Skate Salad with Pickled Vegetables & Lentils

Roasted Spring Lamb Leg with Mint Sauce
& Pot of Jersey Royal Potatoes

Hazelnut & Bitter Chocolate Cake
with Cranberry Sauce

VIN D'ORANGE

Vin d'orange is the prettiest of apéritif drinks. Blush orange-pink in colour and glistening in its clarity, it brings to me memories of warm spring and summer lunches on the southern French coast. Four years ago I was given a recipe for it by the owners of what was one of my most favourite restaurants in Nice, which sadly now has been sold to new owners who have retained the name but have no sense of taste or style. So without them to make it for me, we now make it ourselves.

As soon as the Seville oranges arrive in the London markets from Spain, we macerate the whole sliced fruit in rosé wine and eau-de-vie, and six to eight weeks later, when it is ready, we pour it at the restaurant in champagne glasses as an apéritif. We serve it over ice with a twist of orange peel, usually in small doses, as it is quite alcoholic.

2 small Seville oranges
½ lemon
200g sugar
½ vanilla pod, split lengthwise
¼ cinnamon stick, broken
1 litre good rosé wine
200ml eau-de-vie
50ml rum

Preheat the oven to 180°C/350°F/gas mark 4. Lay a large scrupulously clean jar on a baking sheet and sterilize in the oven for 10 minutes. Boil the lid in a small pan of water for 5 minutes to sterilize.

Wash the skins of the fruit well and slice roughly. Place in the jar with the remaining ingredients except the rum and stir well with a clean stainless-steel spoon. Cover with the lid and refrigerate for 6 weeks, shaking the vessel gently from time to time to dissolve the sugar. Add the rum and pour through a coffee filter into another sterilized bottle. Place a cork into the bottle and serve from the refrigerator. It will last at least a year but I suspect that as it is so delicious it will be gone before spring is out. May I suggest therefore that you make double the quantity to avoid disappointment in the summer?

SALAD OF GLOBE ARTICHOKES & PINK GRAPEFRUIT WITH BLACK OLIVE DRESSING

12–18 small globe artichokes, top quarter trimmed away and stalks cut to 1cm
Maldon salt and pepper
approximately 100ml olive oil
½ tsp chopped thyme leaves
2 large pink grapefruit, peeled with a sharp knife
450g Provençal black olives, stones removed
1 tbsp roughly chopped Italian flat-leaf parsley
3 bunches of landcress or watercress, stalks removed, leaves washed

Bring a pan of salted water to the boil and add the artichokes. Place a smaller lid on top of the artichokes to hold them beneath the surface as they cook. After approximately 12–15 minutes, test with a wooden skewer through the top of the stem: it should feel slightly firm when done. On no account should they be overcooked. Remove from the pan and cool with cold water then drain upside down. Peel the tough outside leaves away until the tender leaves are exposed. Cut each artichoke into halves or quarters, depending on the size, and remove the choke if present. Place in a bowl and season with salt and pepper and the thyme, and a drizzle of the olive oil. Leave to marinate while preparing the remaining ingredients.

Segment the grapefruit carefully and save all excess juice. Chop the olives roughly and mix with enough olive oil to produce a pouring consistency. Add the parsley and season with salt and pepper.

To serve, place the cress leaves in a salad spinner and dry them carefully. Tip them into a bowl and toss with a little olive oil, a drizzle of grapefruit juice, salt and pepper. Arrange neatly on 6 salad plates with grapefruit segments and artichokes tucked amongst the leaves. Spoon the olive dressing around the outside of the salad and serve with grilled toasts or breadsticks (see pages 131 and 192).

POTATO & CHIVE FRITTATA

Frittata is the Italian name for a flat omelette, fried in olive oil and cooked on both sides. It is often served at room temperature or even cold, cut into wedges as an ideal bar snack or picnic food. At the restaurant we often serve it cold with a plate of sliced smoked fish, a small salad of bitter leaves and a scoop of soured cream. Vegetables such as courgette, onion and Swiss chard can be used in addition to or instead of the potatoes.

500g small potatoes (Linzer Delicatesse, Desirée, Roseval, Jersey Royal or Ratte)
60ml olive oil
6 eggs
salt and pepper
2 tbsp chopped chives

Scrub the potatoes and bring them to the boil in a pan of salted water. Simmer until almost tender and drain. Cut them in halves or quarters depending on the size. Preheat an overhead grill to medium.

Heat the olive oil in a 25cm wide heavy non-stick frying pan, add the potatoes and cook them over a high heat until they become golden and crisp. Whisk the eggs together with salt, pepper and the chives and pour them into the pan, spreading the potatoes evenly. Turn down to a medium heat while the frittata continues to cook. Shake the pan occasionally but do not stir the egg; it should be allowed to cook and set undisturbed. When the egg has set around the edge and has begun to rise up slightly and colour, place the pan under the grill and cook until golden. Allow to cool down in the pan. Slide on to a dish and slice as required.

SWEET-SOUR ONIONS

750g small pickling onions
50ml olive oil
1 red chili, sliced fine
2 cloves garlic, crushed to a cream with a little salt
1 tsp chopped thyme leaves
100ml white wine
60ml champagne vinegar or white wine vinegar
50g demerara sugar
¼ tsp salt
2 tbsp chopped Italian flat-leaved parsley
1 tbsp chopped chives

Bring a pan of water to the boil, add the onions and bring back to the boil. Cook for 30 seconds and strain through a colander. With a small sharp knife, remove the outside skins carefully and slice away the hairs of the root.

In a heavy-based pan heat the olive oil gently with the chili, garlic and thyme until they start to sizzle. Add the onions and stir until well coated in the oil. Add the wine, vinegar, sugar and salt and simmer, covered, for 5–10 minutes or until tender. Taste and adjust for seasoning, allow to cool and fold in the parsley and chives.

Serve with cold ham, prosciutto, roasted pork or strong cheeses.

RAVIOLI OF RICOTTA, GOAT'S CHEESE & PARMESAN WITH SAGE & ARTICHOKES

1 recipe Pasta (page 97)

RICOTTA FILLING
180g ricotta
180g soft goat's cheese
4 egg yolks
1 tsp finely chopped sage
½ bunch of chives, finely chopped
salt and pepper
a little melted butter, for brushing the paper
1 egg, whisked, for sealing the ravioli

TO SERVE
12 small globe artichokes
120ml olive oil
50g pinenuts
18 sage leaves
1 clove garlic, crushed to a cream with a little salt
pepper
1 tsp chopped thyme
150g Parmesan shaved with a sharp knife or vegetable peeler

Beat the ricotta, goat's cheese and egg yolks together until smooth. Fold in the sage, chives, salt and pepper. Taste for seasoning, cover and leave refrigerated.

Prepare the artichokes by trimming off the tops by approximately a quarter of the height and trimming the stem to approximately 2 cm in length. Place in a pan of boiling salted water and lay a smaller lid on top to keep the artichokes below the water as they cook. Simmer until a wooden skewer pierces the base easily,

approximately 15 minutes. Drain well, cool and peel away the tough outside leaves to reveal the tender inside. Cut in halves or quarters depending on the size.

To make the ravioli

Roll a quarter of the dough at a time, leaving the remaining dough covered at all times. Using a pasta-rolling machine, roll the dough first on the widest setting, dusting with a scant amount of flour if necessary. Fold the roll in two and roll again. Continue to roll on decreasing settings until it is on the finest setting. Lay the sheet of pasta on a lightly floured table to start to dry. Continue in the same way with the remaining dough. Turn the sheets over from time to time to allow the air to dry both sides. The pasta should remain soft enough to fold but should have a smooth papery feel to it. On no account should it dry completely.

With a sharp 5–5.5 cm biscuit cutter, cut 24 circles from the dough, dusting them with a scant amount of flour to prevent them from sticking together. Lay a sheet of silicone wax paper on a tray or baking sheet and brush lightly with melted butter. On a clean dry board lay half the pasta discs and gently brush the inside rim with a smear of the egg wash. In the centre place a teaspoonful of cheese mixture, and using both hands carefully fold the edges of the pasta together like a Cornish pasty, sealing the edges completely. Place the ravioli on the buttered paper without touching each other. Continue filling the remaining pasta and leave the ravioli in a cool dry place until required. The ravioli are best cooked within 6 hours of being made.

Gently heat three-quarters of the olive oil with the pinenuts. When they have turned golden remove them with a slotted spoon to a small bowl. Add the sage leaves to the pinenut-flavoured oil and cook for a few seconds until crisp, taking care as they may spatter dangerously. Remove the pan from the heat then with a slotted spoon remove the sage leaves and drain them on kitchen paper. Add the garlic, salt and pepper to the oil and pour this over the pinenuts. Leave on one side and keep warm.

To assemble

In a heavy-based frying pan, heat the remaining olive oil and fry the artichokes until just beginning to crisp and turn golden. Season with salt, pepper and thyme and leave in a warm place.

Bring a heavy-based pan of salted water to the boil, turn it down to a simmer and add the ravioli, gently peeling them off the paper. Cook for 2–3 minutes or until the pasta is tender.

Remove the ravioli with a slotted spoon or pour them gently into a colander to drain. Place them into a warm metal or ceramic bowl, and drizzle with a little olive oil, salt and pepper. Toss together carefully as they will be very delicate at this stage.

Divide the artichokes between 6 warm soup plates, place the ravioli on top and spoon over the pinenut oil. Garnish with the sage leaves and shavings of Parmesan.

PASTA

This pasta recipe may also be used to make pasta ribbons, e.g. tagliatelle or linguine, by using the pasta-cutting attachment on the pasta machine. Simply dry the sheets as described above and then carefully feed the pasta through the cutter. It should then be laid loosely on a tray for the cut surfaces to dry a little.

Makes 6 portions – 4 ravioli each

200g pasta flour (00 grade)
a pinch of salt
4 egg yolks
½ beaten egg
10ml olive oil

Place the flour and salt in a mixing bowl. Mix the yolks, egg and olive oil together and pour them in gradually whilst mixing together by hand or with a wooden spoon. This could also be done in a food processor or in a mixer with the dough-hook attachment. Mix until very smooth and shiny; it should feel very firm to the touch. Cover with cling film and allow to rest for at least 1 hour in a cool place, then prepare as directed in the recipe.

FISH CAKES WITH TARTARE SAUCE

1 kg cod fillet or haddock fillet, boned and skinned
1 egg
100g fresh breadcrumbs
1 small red chili, finely chopped
½ tsp salt
zest of 2 lemons
1 tbsp chopped parsley
1 tbsp chopped tarragon
4 spring onions, finely chopped

FOR COATING
100g dried breadcrumbs (see below)
2 eggs
a pinch of salt and pepper

FOR FRYING
60ml vegetable oil

Using the mincing attachment of a mixing machine or the pulse action of a food processor, chop the fish very finely and place in a bowl with the remaining fish cake ingredients. Mix gently but thoroughly and leave in a cool place until required. Form the mixture into patty shapes about 1.5cm thick and lay on a tray sprinkled with a few dried breadcrumbs to prevent them sticking.

Whisk the eggs in a bowl with salt and pepper. In another bowl place the dried breadcrumbs. Using one hand for wet and one hand for dry, coat the fish cakes first with egg, then with breadcrumbs, reshaping them gently if necessary once they are completed.

Heat the vegetable oil in a non-stick pan until a breadcrumb will sizzle vigorously but not burn. Place the fish cakes in the pan gently and fry over a medium heat until dark golden in colour. Turn over and cook again until golden and allow to cook through, approximately 5–6 minutes in total depending on the thickness.

Serve with Mustard Mayonnaise (page 278) or Tartare Sauce (see below).

To make dried breadcrumbs

200g fresh or day old bread

Preheat the oven to 140°C/285°F/gas mark 1.

Cut the bread into walnut-sized pieces and break into crumbs using the sharp blade of the food processor. Spread the breadcrumbs on a baking sheet and bake for up to 15 minutes or until they are almost dry. Use the food processor again to grind them. Once they have cooled they will keep well for 2–3 weeks if stored in a cool place in a sealed container.

TARTARE SAUCE

Mayonnaise made with 250ml olive oil (page 132)
2 tbsp chopped gherkins
1 tbsp whole baby capers, or chopped large capers
1 small red onion, peeled and diced very finely
grated zest and juice of 1 lemon
1 tbsp Dijon mustard
2 tbsp chopped parsley

Mix all ingredients together except the parsley. Taste and adjust the seasoning if necessary. Stir in the parsley just before serving.

WARM SMOKED EEL WITH
CRISP PANCETTA, TREVISSE &
DILL SOURED CREAM

We buy our smoked eel from Norfolk where they are caught in the fresh waters of the River Ouze and River Wensum. They are then smoked to order for us. This is one dish which used to be a hard sell but it appears on menus in various forms throughout the year, although predominately in the spring, and now has more fans than detractors.

1 small smoked eel, approximately 600g, or 400g smoked eel fillets
2 heads trevisse or radicchio, base removed, leaves washed and spun dry in
  a salad spinner
1 tbsp chopped dill
2 tsp chopped Italian flat-leaf parsley
200ml soured cream
½ tbsp Dijon mustard
Maldon salt and pepper
a little olive oil
12 slices pancetta, not too fine
6 small slices of country style bread
a few handfuls of rocket leaves, trimmed of stalks and washed
6 sprigs of parsley
6 lemon wedges

To prepare the eel, first remove the head, then fillet it: lay the eel on a chopping board and with a firm sharp knife kept parallel with the board slice with a sawing action, into the eel over and along the backbone from the head end to the tail. Turn the eel over and remove the second fillet in the same way. Trim away any small bones and then carefully peel the skin off from head to tail. Slice 12 pieces

approximately 4cm wide at an oblique angle and cover with cling film. Leave refrigerated until required.

Cut the trevisse or radicchio into strips about the same width as the eel and leave in a bowl in a cool place.

Mix the dill and parsley with the soured cream, mustard, salt and pepper.

Heat an overhead grill or salamander to the highest heat or an oven to 180°C/350°F/gas mark 4.

In a non-stick pan heat a drizzle of olive oil and fry the pancetta until nearly crisp. Drain on kitchen paper and keep warm.

If using a grill or salamander: place the bread on a baking tray, drizzle with a little olive oil and grill on one side. Turn over and grill again. Remove the toasts and keep warm. Place the trevisse or radicchio in a bowl and drizzle with olive oil, salt and pepper. Toss gently together. Place 6 piles of the trevisse on the baking sheet and then two eel slices on top of each pile and grill for a few moments until the eel is hot and the leaves have wilted.

If using the oven: toast the bread in a toaster, then place the trevisse or radicchio and eel on a baking tray and proceed in the oven as above.

Place the rocket leaves into a bowl and toss with a little olive oil, salt and pepper.

Place the toasts on 6 plates, arrange the rocket on top, then using a fish slice scoop the warm trevisse or radicchio and eel on to the top. Scatter over the crisp pancetta and place a spoonful of dill soured cream on each one. Garnish with parsley sprigs and lemon wedges and serve immediately.

MARINATED FRESH ANCHOVIES

This can only be made with the freshest of fresh anchovies – so go out and find a fisherman! For a generous first course, or as part of a selection of salads for a buffet (for example), select 3–4 anchovies per person. They should be firm to the touch, with glistening eyes and scales, and should have a fresh, appealing smell of the sea. Use approximately ½ a lemon per person.

Wash the anchovies under a cold running tap to remove the scales, for it is surprising how large the scales are for these tiny fish. Make a small incision in the belly and remove the innards. Rinse under cold running water. Dry the fish with kitchen paper and lay them on a chopping board. With a small sharp knife, slide the blade over the backbone from the base of the head to the tail. The fillet should come away from the bone with one easy stroke as they are so tender. Turn the fish over and remove the second fillet in the same way. Once they are all filleted, wipe the flesh side with kitchen paper and check that no bones remain. Discard the debris. Choose a flat platter to display the anchovies on and sprinkle with half the lemon juice. Lay the anchovies neatly in tight rows on top of this, silver skin up, and then sprinkle with the remaining lemon juice. Cover with cling film and chill for at least 1 hour.

To serve, drizzle with good olive oil, sprinkle with chopped parsley and serve chilled with grilled or toasted brown bread, radishes and lemon wedges.

SKATE SALAD WITH PICKLED VEGETABLES & LENTILS

FOR THE MARINADE
30ml champagne wine vinegar
grated zest and juice of 1 orange
90ml olive oil
½ small chili, chopped fine, with seeds
a pinch of Maldon salt

FOR THE SALAD
4 large carrots, peeled, halved and sliced fine
8 sticks celery, washed and sliced fine
2 fennel bulbs, washed, halved and sliced fine
360g Puy or Castelluccio lentils
½ tsp salt
2 bay leaves
1 tsp chopped thyme leaves
2 tsp chopped parsley leaves
3 tbsp balsamic vinegar
90ml olive oil
a pinch of Maldon salt
½ small chili, chopped fine with seeds
6 small skate wings, approximately 200g each
2 litres Vegetable Stock (pages 37–8) or 1 litre Fish Stock (see page 38) and 1 litre water

TO SERVE
2 tbsp celery leaves, chopped roughly
2 tbsp coriander leaves, chopped roughly
6 sprigs coriander

Mix the marinade ingredients together in a medium-sized bowl. Bring a pan of salted water to the boil and plunge the prepared carrots, celery and fennel for 10–20 seconds to blanch. Drain thoroughly and immediately toss into the marinade, gently stirring as it cools. Leave on one side. Place the lentils in a small pan and cover with water to twice their depth. Add the salt and bay leaves, bring to the boil and simmer for 8–10 minutes or until the lentils are tender but not broken. Drain and rinse with cold water. Mix the thyme, parsley, balsamic vinegar and olive oil together with salt and the chili. Add the lentils and toss together gently.

Rinse the skate wings thoroughly and place in a wide shallow cooking vessel (we use a roasting tray at the restaurant). Pour the vegetable stock or fish stock and water into the pan, bring to a gentle simmer and cook until the fish flakes easily away from the cartilage, approximately 6–8 minutes. Allow it to cool in the liquid. Keep the liquid to use for a fish soup or stew.

To serve, fold the celery and coriander leaves into the drained pickled vegetables and divide between 6 serving plates. Carefully peel the skate meat away from the cartilage in pieces and lay it over the vegetables. Spoon the lentils over and garnish with coriander sprigs.

ROASTED SPRING LAMB LEG WITH MINT SAUCE & POT OF JERSEY ROYAL POTATOES

Although it would be difficult and wasteful to serve a roasted leg of lamb on the bone at the restaurant, this is one of my favourite dishes for cooking at home. At home it is easy to serve chunks of meat carved away from the bone at odd angles, whereas at the restaurant we prefer to bone out the leg first, thus allowing the carving to be more straightforward and the sizing of portions more even.

Try to choose a leg of lamb from a quality butcher who knows its provenance.

2.2kg leg of lamb, bone in
80ml olive oil
1 tbsp chopped rosemary
salt and pepper
2 large carrots, peeled and chopped roughly
1 onion, peeled and chopped roughly
3 sticks celery, chopped roughly
1 head of garlic, chopped roughly
small sprigs of bay, rosemary and thyme
750g Jersey Royal potatoes, washed
1 tsp flour
½ bottle red wine
500ml Lamb Stock, or Chicken or Vegetable Stock (pages 38 and 39)
1 tbsp Redcurrant, Apple and Rosemary Jelly (page 179)
50g butter, melted
Maldon salt and pepper
1 tbsp chopped tarragon, parsley or chives

Preheat the oven to 190°C/375°F/gas mark 5.

With a small sharp knife trim away a little of the excess fat from the lamb and place the fat in the roasting tin. With the same knife criss-cross the top and sides of the leg fat, making shallow incisions. Mix half the olive oil with the rosemary, salt and pepper and rub this in by hand over the fat and into the slashes.

Place the roasting tin over a medium heat and warm the fat with the remaining olive oil for a few seconds. Add the vegetables and herbs and stir occasionally until golden brown. Add the lamb leg and turn over in the hot oil until it begins to colour. Sprinkle with a little extra salt and roast in the oven for 30 minutes or until the fat starts to brown. Remove it from the oven and turn the temperature down to 160°C/325°F/gas mark 3. Scrape the vegetables away from the bottom of the pan and turn the lamb over. Baste with a little of the fat and continue to roast for 45–50 minutes. Test by inserting a metal skewer into the thickest part of the leg: for a medium rare result the tip should feel warm to the touch. Remove the lamb to a serving dish and cover loosely with foil and then two tea towels. This will prevent too much heat escaping and will allow the lamb to relax whilst the gravy is made and potatoes cooked.

Bring the potatoes to the boil in salted water and cook until just tender. They should retain a touch of firmness.

Meanwhile, place the roasting pan back on a medium heat and skim away a little of the excess oil. Sprinkle with the flour and stir constantly, scraping the darkened vegetables away from the pan. Add the wine and the stock and simmer until the gravy thickens and colours. Taste and add salt and pepper if necessary. Finally add the redcurrant jelly, return to the boil and strain.

Drain the potatoes, toss in melted butter, season with Maldon salt and pepper and place in a serving dish or 6 small individual pots which will sit on each dinner plate. Sprinkle with the herbs. Unwrap the lamb, slice and serve with mint sauce and the hot gravy on the side.

MINT SAUCE

150g shallots, finely diced
45ml balsamic vinegar
90ml olive oil
Maldon salt and pepper
6 tbsp chopped fresh mint leaves

Mix all the ingredients together except the mint and allow to infuse for at least 30 minutes. Add the mint, taste for seasoning and serve.

HAZELNUT & BITTER CHOCOLATE CAKE WITH CRANBERRY SAUCE

Makes 1 cake of 10–12 slices

40g hazelnuts
250g unsalted butter, plus a small amount melted for brushing the tin
255g bitter chocolate
200g caster sugar
6 eggs, separated
50g flour

FOR THE CHOCOLATE COATING
200g bitter chocolate
100g unsalted butter
50ml double cream

Preheat the oven to 160°C/325°F/gas mark 3. Roast the hazelnuts and peel them by rubbing their skins gently with a cloth, then chop them finely.

Brush a 22cm cake tin with melted butter. Place a disc of greaseproof or silicone wax paper in the base to prevent sticking.

Melt the butter and chocolate over a pan of hot water and let it cool slightly. Mix three-quarters of the sugar with the yolks until well blended, and fold in the chocolate mixture. Stir in the flour and hazelnuts. Whisk the whites with the remaining sugar until soft peaks are formed and fold this carefully but thoroughly into the chocolate mixture.

Pour into the prepared cake tin and bake for 40–50 minutes. Test by piercing a wooden skewer into the centre of the cake: it should be clean when removed. Cool in the tin. Carefully slide a small knife around the rim of the cake and turn it upside down on to a cooling rack.

To make the chocolate coating, melt the chocolate and butter over a pan of hot water. Bring the cream to a boil and mix into the chocolate.

Place a large plate under the cooling rack and pour the warm chocolate mixture over the top of the cake; allow the mixture to fall over and down the sides evenly by gently pushing the warm chocolate with the base of a spoon. The plate will catch any drips. Leave the chocolate to set in a cool place. Serve within 2 days just as it is with whipped cream or with Cranberry Sauce.

CRANBERRY SAUCE

300g fresh or frozen cranberries, discoloured ones removed
juice of 2 large oranges
100g sugar
icing sugar, to taste

Cook the cranberries with the orange juice and sugar over a gentle heat until soft (approximately 10 minutes).

Pass through a sieve and sweeten with icing sugar to taste.

SUMMER

GARDEN PICNIC LUNCH

Soup of Five Tomatoes & Three Beetroots

Rocket Leaf & Herb Focaccia

Salade Niçoise

Cracked Wheat Salad

Grilled Chicken Salad with Three Peppers,
Lemon, Capers & Basil

Fresh Goat's Cheese with Salad of Herbs

Apricot & Almond Tart

Lavender Shortbread

SOUP OF FIVE TOMATOES & THREE BEETROOTS

Over the years we have met a variety of smallholders and gardeners who have been able to supply us with a wide range of summer fruits and vegetables. In particular, the range of both tomatoes and beetroots has been extraordinary! From the large ugly bulbous red- and orange-fleshed tomatoes of southern Italy and Sicily to the dainty strings of 'cherry' tomatoes grown both in Britain and on the Continent, we have made some stunningly beautiful salads, soups and tarts.

I do not have a clear memory of how or when the idea for this chilled soup first materialized, but I know that it was placed on a dinner menu in a blisteringly hot summer a few years ago and because of its freshness and acidity, it became an instant success and has gained a firm place on our summer menus, both for lunch and dinner.

If the large red cooked beetroot is the only type available, peel and trim the outsides, creating a cube shape, and use the trimmings in the base of the soup. The remaining cube should then be cut either into matchsticks or into small dice and tossed with the selection of tomatoes as described.

FOR THE SOUP BASE
90 ml olive oil
½ head new season garlic, roughly chopped
1 large onion, peeled and roughly chopped
4 stalks celery, washed and roughly chopped
1 fennel, washed and roughly chopped
500g very ripe plum tomatoes, washed and roughly chopped
500g very ripe beefsteak tomatoes, washed and roughly chopped
250g medium to large red beetroot, cooked, peeled and roughly chopped
2 tbsp chopped basil, plus the stalks
Maldon salt
pepper

FOR THE GARNISH

50g of two types of baby beetroot — any colour or shape,
    e.g. red, yellow, pink, round, long
1 tbsp long cut chives, 2 cm long
good olive oil
120g of three types of tomatoes — any colour or shape,
    e.g. cherry red, cherry yellow, tear shaped, orange
120 ml crème fraiche (optional)
6 sprigs of basil

Preheat the oven to 200°C/400°F/gas mark 6.

In a heavy-based pan gently heat the olive oil with the garlic, onion, celery and fennel and cook them until they start to soften without browning. Add the tomatoes, beetroot, basil stalks, salt and pepper. Barely cover with water, bring to the boil, and then place uncovered in the oven for 40 minutes or until all vegetables are tender. Liquidize, adding a little water if necessary, and pass through a sieve pushing the debris with the underside of a ladle until almost dry. Taste for seasoning, check consistency and chill in the refrigerator.

Cook the garnish beetroot in two separate pans of boiling salted water until tender, approximately 20–25 minutes. Drain, cool and peel under running cold water. Trim the tails and tops of the beetroot and cut into halves or quarters depending on their size. If using different-coloured beetroot, keep the yellow and red in separate bowls so the colours do not stain. Season each bowl with a quarter of the basil leaves and chives, salt, pepper and a drizzle of olive oil. Cut each type of garnish tomato depending on its shape and size: some may need to be quartered whilst others may be small enough to keep whole. Place together in a bowl, and season as before with the remaining basil and chives.

If at home, place 6 soup plates or bowls in the freezer at least 1 hour before serving. If out on a picnic, try to store the soup plates in a cool bag until required.

To serve, stir the soup well, check the seasoning and half fill each bowl. Spoon into the centre of each dish the tomatoes and beetroots. Garnish with the basil sprigs, a drizzle of good olive oil and a generous scoop of crème fraiche if using.

ROCKET LEAF & HERB FOCACCIA

200g strong plain flour
a pinch of salt
10g fresh yeast or 5g dried yeast
50ml olive oil and extra for drizzling
warm water
1 tsp chopped thyme
1 small bunch of rocket leaves
Maldon salt

Mix the flour and salt together. Blend the yeast with a dash of warm water, mix until smooth and add to the flour. Add 50ml olive oil and enough warm water to produce a soft dough. Add the thyme and knead gently until smooth. This may be done by hand, or in a mixer with the dough-hook on the slowest speed. Place in a lightly oiled bowl, cover with cling film and leave in a warm place to prove until it has doubled in bulk. Preheat the oven to 190°C/375°F/gas mark 5.

Remove the dough from the bowl and knead again until smooth. Shape into a smooth ball and then roll into a disc approximately 1cm thick and place on a well-oiled baking sheet. Drizzle with olive oil and cover with cling film. Leave in a warm draught-free place to rise for 15–20 minutes.

Toss the rocket in olive oil as for a salad and scatter over the top of the focaccia with a little Maldon salt. Press your fingertips into the dough lightly to press the rocket on to the dough. This will also create the characteristic dimple marks. Bake for 20–25 minutes until risen and golden. Remove from the oven and drizzle with a little extra olive oil.

A variety of herbs or spices may be substituted in this focaccia recipe by replacing the thyme and rocket with one or more of the following: 1 chili chopped very fine, 1 tbsp fine-chopped rosemary, 2 tbsp chopped dill.

SALADE NIÇOISE

What is a Salade Niçoise? Turn to dozens of accomplished and revered writers of food history and you will find a diverse set of opinions. Elizabeth David places tuna, potatoes and green beans as optional extras in her book *French Provincial Cooking*, listing tomatoes, olives, anchovy fillets and hard-boiled eggs as essentials. Colman Andrews, writing in his wonderfully enticing book *Flavors of the Riviera*, calls his Salade Niçoise 'La (Vraie) Salade Niçoise', adding cucumber and green peppers to his list. Lovely Simon Hopkinson has yet another suggestion, that tuna is an unnecessary ingredient but that gallons of anchovies are! So many battles have been fought over the authenticity of individual recipes and yet, does it really matter? I feel that as long as the main ingredients are correct, and that it radiates with all the elements of Nice – the sea, the sun and the freshness and vitality of their raw ingredients – then who should care what goes into the salad bowl?

Here is mine, anyway – just make sure that the tomatoes are ripe!

1 x 500g piece of blue fin tuna fillet
4 tbsp olive oil
1 clove garlic, crushed to a cream with a little salt
pepper
12 quails' eggs
300g fine green beans
18 radishes, with leaves attached
300g cherry tomatoes on the vine or a selection of different shapes and colours of tomatoes
1 small cos lettuce
1 small escarole lettuce
½ bunch of chives, cut 2–3cm long
a few small sprigs of parsley
good olive oil
Maldon salt
pepper

350g new potatoes, cooked in the skin, cut in halves or quarters, depending on size
12 fillets of salted anchovy
200g Niçoise olives
Roasted Garlic Mayonnaise (page 57) made with 250ml olive oil
6 lemon wedges

Preheat the oven to 200°C/400°F/gas mark 6.

Trim away and discard any dark red parts of the tuna, and lay it on a plate. Mix the oil with the garlic and pepper and smear this over the surface of the tuna. Place a non-stick ovenproof frying pan over a medium heat, put in the tuna and cook on one side until it is sealed and begins to colour. Turn it over until all surfaces are sealed. Roast in the oven until medium rare, approximately 10–15 minutes, depending on the thickness of the fillet. Test by piercing it with a metal skewer: the tip should feel warm when removed from the centre. Allow to cool.

Place the quails' eggs in a small pan, cover with water and bring to the boil, then immediately cool under cold running water and drain. Do not peel the eggs – their shells are too beautiful for your guests not to see!

Trim the tops from the beans and leave the tails on. Blanch in boiling salted water for a few seconds, until they have just lost their natural crispness. Strain, and lay the beans on a tray to cool rapidly.

Trim the radishes of any unsightly leaves and soak them in a bowl of cold water until required.

Snip the tomatoes from vine into small sprigs, allowing 3–4 tomatoes per person. Alternatively, wash a selection of tomatoes and cut in half if necessary.

Remove the outside leaves of the cos and escarole lettuces and wash the hearts. Break the leaves into similar sized pieces and spin in a salad spinner. Place in a large salad bowl with the chives and parsley.

To serve, drizzle olive oil over the leaves, season with salt and pepper and toss gently. Arrange on 6 chilled salad plates. In another bowl toss the potato, green beans, and cut tomatoes if using, with a little olive oil, salt and pepper as before. Place on top of the leaves. Slice the tuna with a sharp knife or break the fillet gently in its natural flakes. Arrange the tuna on leaves with the radishes, quails' eggs, vine tomatoes if using, and the anchovy fillets and olives. Spoon a generous amount of roasted garlic mayonnaise to one side and serve with a lemon wedge.

Preheat a grill or salamander to the highest setting (see grilling notes on page 170).

Trim the bases from each pepper and remove the seeds. Slice off the 3 or 4 sides in as large pieces as possible. Grill with the skin sides towards the flame until they are black. Remove to a bowl and cover to steam and cool. Peel carefully and cut the flesh into large triangles. Place in a bowl with the capers, olive oil, lemon zest, salt and chili, and gently stir. Leave on one side.

Mix the chopped basil, garlic and olive oil together and spread over the flesh side of the chicken. Place the chicken on the grill, skin-side down, and grill until seared, then turn 90° to criss-cross the bar marks and grill until golden. Turn over and cook through, approximately 3–5 minutes, testing with a skewer. The juices should run clear, not pink, when cooked. Remove the chicken to a board, slice it into 1 cm strips and add them with the parsley and small basil leaves to the peppers, then toss them gently together. Taste for seasoning and serve either immediately or chilled.

FRESH GOAT'S CHEESE
WITH SALAD OF HERBS

The fragility of this salad demands careful preparation and immediate serving once it has been arranged.

Instead of tossing the leaves in a dressing as one would do normally, I prefer to drizzle the olive oil over the plate at the last second to avoid unnecessary handing of the delicate leaves. Any soft fresh goat's cheese would be perfect for this salad.

½ curly endive lettuce
½ bunch of Italian flat-leaf parsley
½ bunch of chives
1 small bunch of chervil

1 small bunch of dill
¼ bunch of coriander
12 nasturtium leaves
a selection of edible blossoms, e.g. pansies and nasturtiums
salt and pepper
good olive oil
50–75 g goat's cheese per person

Carefully tear the endive apart, wash in cold water and dry in a salad spinner.

Pick the parsley into small sprigs, wash and dry as above. Cut the chives into 2cm lengths, and pick the chervil, dill, coriander and nasturtium leaves into small sprigs. Toss the endive together with the herbs and place in a salad bowl, cover with cling film and chill in a refrigerator for at least 30 minutes before serving.

On chilled plates arrange the herb salad and arrange the blossoms amongst them attractively. Sprinkle with a little salt and pepper and drizzle with olive oil. Slice a selection of fresh goat's cheeses, place them to one side of the salad and serve immediately.

APRICOT & ALMOND TART

Living in London as I do, there is one view of Paris which I desperately miss, and that is the sight of a partially burnt apricot or peach tart in the window of a good bakery. There is something unashamed and at the same time proud about the fruit tarts which are displayed in every neighbourhood patisserie, always singed, always crusty and enticing. Make sure this one has some burnt edges to it.

FOR THE SWEET PASTRY
120g flour
a pinch of salt
60g butter, chilled and cubed
40g sugar
1 tbsp water
1 egg yolk

FOR THE FILLING
80g soft butter
80g caster sugar
40g almonds, chopped medium fine
40g ground almonds
1 egg
50g flour

FOR THE APRICOTS
750g apricots, halved and stoned
25g caster sugar
icing sugar

Sieve the flour and salt and rub in the butter until it resembles fine breadcrumbs. Stir in the sugar and add the water and egg yolk, mixing gently until the mixture comes together. Gently knead it for a few moments until it begins to look smooth. Wrap it and chill it for at least 1 hour. Roll it out and fill a 24cm fluted tart tin, pressing the pastry well into the ribs. Chill it again for 30 minutes and preheat the oven to 180°C/350°F/gas mark 4.

Line the pastry with a disc of greaseproof or silicone wax paper and fill it with baking beans. Bake for 15–20 minutes and remove the paper. Continue to bake for 5–6 minutes or until the pastry is golden on the base.

Meanwhile make the almond filling. Cream the butter and sugar until soft and light. Beat in the almonds and ground almonds, then the egg and finally the flour.

Spread the almond filling into the cooled pastry. Standing the apricot halves upright next to one another, fill the tart in circles starting from the outside working inwards. Sprinkle with the caster sugar and bake for 20 minutes or until the edges of the apricots have started to singe, then turn the oven temperature down to 160°C/325°F/gas mark 3 and continue to cook for 30 minutes or until the almond cream has cooked through. Dust with icing sugar and serve.

LAVENDER SHORTBREAD

These unusual fragrantly flavoured biscuits are a perfect accompaniment to many summer desserts, or just by themselves at teatime.

For 24 crescent-shaped biscuits

1 tsp finely chopped lavender blossoms (approximately 3 lavender heads)
100g caster sugar
200g unsalted butter
300g flour
a pinch of salt

Mix the lavender with the sugar then lightly cream it with the butter. Sieve the flour with the salt and mix together with the butter and sugar to make a soft dough. Chill for at least 1 hour.

Preheat the oven to 160°C/325°F/gas mark 3. Roll the dough out approximately 5mm thick and cut into crescents using a 8cm fluted cutter. Place on a baking sheet, sprinkle with a little caster sugar and bake for 15–20 minutes or until pale golden. They will become crisp on cooling. When cool store in an airtight container for up to 4 days.

SUPPER

Salad of Basil-Roasted Aubergine with
Buffalo Mozzarella & Country Bread Toasts

Poached Sea Trout with Chive
& Nasturtium Blossom Mayonnaise

Summer Vegetables

Herbed Wild Rice

Summer Berry Trifle

SALAD OF BASIL-ROASTED AUBERGINE WITH BUFFALO MOZZARELLA & COUNTRY BREAD TOASTS

We are very fortunate in having an Italian supplier of fresh hand-shaped buffalo milk mozzarella who is able to deliver to us twice a week, throughout the year, directly from Rome. But it is by no accident that this wonderful product arrives in such perfect condition. A friend of my supplier's family owns the buffalo farm and another friend makes the cheese for him, which allows the milk to be checked at regular intervals during its production to make sure that no tampering with the product occurs. From the farm to the cheese factory to the packing area and then on to the airport it is guarded. In this way I can be assured of a true buffalo-milk product with no additives. Sadly, too often, mozzarella has been cheapened by the addition of cow's milk, resulting in an inferior product, rubbery and bland, good only for cheap pizzas in cheap restaurants. Slice into the two cheeses to compare and there will be no hesitation in your verdict. The whiteness, sweetness and softness of the real thing cannot be mistaken. As the cheese is cut open the milky fluids will start to flow, and it needs simply a sprinkling of flaked Maldon salt, a crack of pepper and a drizzle of fruity olive oil.

Serve this glorious white cheese on a plain white plate as they do in Capri, in little family run restaurants in the hills, shaded by the lemon trees . . .

Alternatively make the following:

3 medium-sized firm aubergines
60ml olive oil, plus a little for drizzling and the salad
2 bunches of basil, stalks removed, leaves roughly chopped
2 cloves garlic, crushed to a cream with 1 tsp Maldon salt
pepper
6 balls of mozzarella
Maldon sea salt
150g rocket leaves, trimmed of large stalks, washed and spun in a salad spinner
6 lemon wedges

Heat a grill or salamander to its highest setting (see grilling notes, page 170).

Cut the aubergines in half lengthwise, through the stalk also. Make two or three criss-cross incisions into the flesh with a sharp knife approximately half the depth of the aubergine. Drizzle with a little olive oil and grill at an angle on the cut side until golden. Move the aubergines 90° to cross the bar markings and cook until they are a deep golden-brown colour, approximately 3–4 minutes. If using a salamander, grill until they turn a deep golden colour. Remove to a baking sheet and place cut-side up. Mix the basil, garlic, olive oil and pepper to a paste, spread equally over each aubergine half and leave to marinate for at least half an hour. Preheat the oven to 180°C/350°F/gas mark 4.

Bake for 10–12 minutes or until gently sizzling.

Drain the mozzarella balls, cut them in quarters and sprinkle with salt and pepper. Toss the rocket leaves in a bowl with more olive oil, salt and pepper and arrange on salad plates with the aubergines. Pile the mozzarella on top, garnish with lemon wedges and serve with the Country Bread Toasts.

COUNTRY BREAD

500g strong white flour, plus a little for dusting
15g salt
15g fresh yeast or 7g dried yeast
300ml warm water
a little medium-ground cornmeal

Mix the flour with the salt in a mixing bowl. In a small bowl mix the yeast with half the warm water until the yeast becomes liquid. On a slow speed and with the dough-hook attachment mix the liquid into the flour gradually until a soft dough is formed, adding the remaining water when needed. Continue to mix for 5–8 minutes or until the dough is smooth and shiny. Alternatively the mixing can be done by hand in a medium-sized bowl and the dough turned out on to a clean table and kneaded for 5–10 minutes until smooth.

Place the dough in a clean bowl, cover with cling film and allow to rise in a warm place until doubled in bulk. This may take up to 1 hour depending on the temperature of the kitchen and the weather.

Preheat the oven to 180°C/350°F/gas mark 4 and sprinkle a baking sheet with a little cornmeal.

Place the dough on a clean table and knead again until smooth to expel the air. Shape into 2 balls and with a rolling pin roll the dough into 2 round shapes approximately 15cm across and 2cm high. Lift on to the baking sheet, dust lightly with white flour and cover with cling film. Allow to rise again, approximately half again in size. Remove the plastic and with a very sharp knife slash the surface of the dough in 5 or 6 criss-cross markings and place immediately in the oven. Turn up the heat to 205°C/400°F/gas mark 5 and bake for approximately 25–30 minutes or until it is crisp and golden and sounds hollow when the base is gently knocked. Cool and use within 2 days.

COUNTRY BREAD TOASTS

1 loaf country bread or similar plain bread, preferably 1 day old
olive oil
2 tsp chopped thyme leaves
rock salt and pepper

Heat the oven to 180°C/350°F/gas mark 4.

Slice the loaf as finely as possible (we use the ham-slicing machine). Lay the slices on a baking sheet, drizzle with a fine stream of olive oil, and sprinkle with thyme, salt and pepper. Bake in the oven for approximately 10–12 minutes or until crisp and dry. Alternatively, they may be grilled under a salamander until golden, turned over and grilled again. If some of the edges become slightly singed, all the better.

POACHED SEA TROUT WITH CHIVE & NASTURTIUM BLOSSOM MAYONNAISE

FOR THE MAYONNAISE
1 egg and 1 egg yolk, free range or organic
250ml olive oil
juice of 1 lemon
Maldon salt and pepper
approximately 16 nasturtium blossoms with tender leaves attached
½ bunch of chives, chopped small

FOR THE SEA TROUT
1 x 900g −1kg sea trout fillet, skin left on, carefully boned with tweezers
2 litres Vegetable Stock (page 37)
6 lemon wedges

Place the egg and yolk in a bowl and add the olive oil drop by drop whisking until a thick emulsion is achieved. The oil may be added more rapidly when half has been used. If it becomes too thick to handle easily, add a drop or two of lemon juice, then continue with the remaining oil. Add salt, pepper and more lemon juice to taste.

Choose 6 perfect nasturtium blossoms and keep them on one side. Chop the remaining flowers and leaves roughly with a sharp knife. Just before serving, fold into the mayonnaise with the chives.

Slice the sea trout fillet into 6 even-sized portions.

In a heavy-based roasting tin or shallow cast-iron dish, bring the stock to a simmer. Lower the fillets into the liquid and gently poach for 5−10 minutes. The time will depend on the thickness of the fillet. Test the doneness by pressing the flesh carefully. It should feel slightly firm to the touch.

Remove the fish from the broth and peel away the skin. Arrange the pieces on the serving plates with a little mayonnaise spooned over the top. Garnish with the reserved blossoms and the lemon wedges and serve the remaining mayonnaise separately with summer vegetables and herbed wild rice.

SUMMER VEGETABLES

Choose a selection from the young small vegetables listed below that complement each other in colour, texture and shape. Once they have been prepared, they may be left for up to 1 hour, in separate bowls of cold water to keep fresh until cooking. Otherwise keep them in separate plastic bags in the refrigerator.

3 bay leaves
asparagus, trimmed of tough ends and rinsed
spring cabbage hearts, the tender inside leaves only
carrots, orange or yellow, scrubbed well or peeled if necessary, keeping 1–2cm of green
    top attached
courgettes, small, both ends trimmed at an angle, cut in half lengthwise and washed
leeks, no thicker than an index finger, trimmed of the root end carefully so that just the
    hairs are removed, then cut to the desired length on an angle (keep the trimmings of
    the green end for other uses such as stocks or soups)
fennel, small, trimmed of the outside leaf and base, cut into halves or quarters
green, yellow or purple beans, the top, not the tail, trimmed off, and washed
olive oil
salt and pepper

Bring a large pan of salted water to the boil and add the bay leaves. Add the firmest vegetables (beans, carrots, fennel) first and cook for 1–2 minutes or until they just begin to cook through. Add the remaining vegetables and continue to boil until al dente. Cabbage heart leaves may be added at the last second. Strain the vegetables into a colander and then place immediately in a bowl. Add a generous drizzle of olive oil, salt and pepper, toss gently and arrange in a bowl or on individual plates, taking care to share the colours and shapes evenly.

HERBED WILD RICE

200g wild rice
salt
2 bay leaves
60ml olive oil
Maldon salt and pepper
1 tbsp chopped chervil
1 tbsp chopped Italian flat-leaf parsley
1 tbsp small-chopped chives

Place the rice in a heavy-based pan and cover it to three times its depth with water. Add salt and the bay leaves. Bring to the boil and simmer until just tender, approximately 8–10 minutes. The grains should retain a slight 'bite'. On no account must they split. Drain and place them in a bowl with the olive oil, salt, pepper and herbs. Toss together and serve either immediately or at room temperature.

SUMMER BERRY TRIFLE

1 sheet of Génoise sponge cake (page 137)
250 ml Crème anglaise (page 137)
300 ml double cream, lightly whipped
200 g strawberries
200 g raspberries
200 g tayberries
200 g loganberries
200 g black, red and white currants
a little sugar
a squeeze of lemon juice or sweet white wine
90 g unsalted shelled pistachio nuts, roughly chopped
6 mint sprigs

Cut the cake into even-sized diamond shapes or cubes. Each portion will require 5 or 6 pieces.

Mix the crème anglaise and cream together gently.

Choose the best berries out of half of each type of the fruits and keep 6 beautiful sprays of the redcurrants. Remove the remaining currants from their stalks and place them with the remainder of the berries in a liquidizer or food processor with a scant amount of sugar and a little lemon juice or sweet white wine. Purée until smooth and pass through a plastic sieve. Taste for sharpness. It must not taste too sweet.

Chill 6 soup plates or bowls. Place the cake around the inside of the bowls. Toss the reserved fruits with half the purée and spoon into the centre. Pour the cream mixture over the cake and sprinkle this with the nuts. Pour the remaining purée over the fruit and decorate with mint.

GÉNOISE SPONGE CAKE

vegetable oil
3 eggs
85g caster sugar
85g flour, sieved twice
25g unsalted butter, melted and cooled
½ tsp vanilla extract

Preheat the oven to 180°C/350°F/gas mark 4. Brush a baking sheet approximately 20 cm x 28 cm x 2 cm with vegetable oil and line with silicone wax paper. Whisk the eggs with the sugar until very thick and creamy. Gently fold in the flour, followed by the butter, until smooth. Immediately pour into the prepared tin and bake for 10–12 minutes or until a wooden skewer comes away clean when inserted into the centre. Cool in the tin.

CRÈME ANGLAISE

Makes 250ml

1 vanilla pod
200ml milk
3 egg yolks
65g sugar

Split the vanilla pod in two lengthwise and place in a small pan with the milk. Infuse over a very low heat for at least 10 minutes, without boiling. In a bowl mix the yolks with the sugar to a paste. Pour the hot milk and vanilla into the bowl and stir continuously until smooth. Return to the pan and stir with a wooden spoon over a very gentle heat until it begins to thicken, without boiling. It will coat the back of a spoon when ready (about 8 minutes). Strain the custard into a bowl and allow it to cool over a bowl of iced water. The vanilla pod may be used a second time if rinsed well and then dried.

DINNER

Plaited Herb & Olive Oil Bread

Jellied Broth with Summer Vegetables,
Fromage Frais & Blossoms

Roasted Wild Scottish Salmon with Young Spinach,
Girolles & Courgette-Flower Fritters

Cashel Blue with Cherries

Raspberry & Nectarine Brioche with
Rich Vanilla Cream

PLAITED HERB & OLIVE OIL BREAD

500g strong white flour, plus a little for dusting
10g salt
10g fresh yeast or 5g dried yeast
250ml warm water
50ml olive oil, plus a little extra for brushing
2 tbsp finely sliced green tops of spring onion
1 tsp chopped thyme
1 tsp chopped parsley
½ tsp Maldon salt

Mix the flour with the salt in a bowl. In a small bowl mix the yeast with half the warm water until the yeast has become liquid. Add the olive oil. Pour the liquid into the flour and mix until a soft dough is formed adding the remaining water if necessary. Continue to mix until a smooth shiny dough is formed. Alternatively the mixing can be done by hand and then turned out on to a clean table, dusted with a little flour and kneaded for 5–10 minutes until smooth.

Place the dough in a clean bowl which has been smeared with a little olive oil, cover with cling film and leave in a warm place for up to 1 hour or until the dough has doubled in bulk.

Preheat the oven to 160°C/325°F/gas mark 3 and brush two 20cm x 10cm loaf tins with olive oil.

Remove the dough from the bowl and place it on a table dusted with a little flour. Sprinkle over the spring onion and herbs and knead these into the dough, expelling the air in the dough at the same time. Roll into 2 short fat sausage shapes approximately 20cm long. Preparing 1 loaf at a time, cut the dough almost completely into 3 lengthwise, leaving approximately 3cm at one end intact. Plait the 3 strands together and tuck the cut ends underneath the loaf neatly. Place the loaves into the tins carefully with the cut ends underneath. Brush the dough with a little more olive oil, cover with cling film and leave in a warm place to rise to half its size again. This will take up to 30 minutes.

Sprinkle the dough with a little Maldon salt and place on the middle shelf of the oven. Turn up the heat to 180°C/350°F/gas mark 4 and bake until golden, approximately 30–35 minutes. Raising the oven temperature will help the initial raising of the soft dough before the crust is formed. Turn out the loaves and check that the loaf sounds hollow when the base is knocked. Brush the loaves with a little extra olive oil, cool and use within 2 days.

Jellied Broth with Summer Vegetables, Fromage Frais & Blossoms

Chilled consommé is generally associated with the elderly or invalids but this dish is full of flavour, texture and vitality. In fact it is as much a salad as a soup. For best results, serve it in soup plates which have been chilled for at least 1 hour in a fridge or freezer. In this way the broth will retain its set, and the vegetables and herbs their freshness.

For the consommé

2 carrots, peeled and washed
1 large onion, peeled
1 leek, trimmed, sliced in half lengthwise, and washed
4 stalks celery, washed
1 fennel, cut in half and washed
50g butter
3 bay leaves
1 small spray each of thyme, rosemary, sage, parsley
6 peppercorns
½ bottle red wine
1.5 litres good chicken or meat stock, slightly set, skimmed of any fat

Cut all the vegetables into hazelnut-sized pieces. In a heavy-based pan heat the butter until foaming, add the vegetables, and cook until they just begin to brown. Add the herbs, peppercorns and wine and bring to the boil. Add the stock and place the pan over half the heat source. Bring to a simmer, skimming often with a ladle. Reduce by half. Taste, strain into a jug through a fine-meshed cloth and allow to cool. Remove any remaining fat from the surface then pour almost all the liquid into a shallow tray or dish. Discard the last few drops as they may contain solids which will cloud the broth. Cover and refrigerate until set.

For the summer vegetables

Choose a selection of vegetables to complement each other in colour, texture and shape. A total weight of approximately 900g of the prepared vegetables is required.

asparagus tips and stalks, cut into 2cm lengths on the angle
young carrots, scrubbed, rinsed, and sliced on an angle
young courgettes, tops and bottoms removed and sliced on an angle
peas, podded
broad beans, podded, blanched for 5 seconds, plunged into iced water and skins removed
1 tbsp chopped tarragon
1 tbsp finely chopped chives
30ml olive oil
Maldon salt and pepper

FOR THE FROMAGE FRAIS
200g fromage frais
½ tbsp finely chopped tarragon
½ tbsp finely chopped chives

FOR THE GARNISH
sprays of tarragon
a few long (2cm) chopped chives
a few chive blossoms snipped from the head with small scissors

Bring a pan of salted water to the boil and plunge all the vegetables except the broad beans into the water. Remove with a slotted spoon after a few seconds and put on a tray to cool. When completely cold place in a bowl with the prepared broad beans, herbs, olive oil, salt and pepper. Toss gently. Mix the fromage frais with its herbs and season.

To serve

Spoon the jellied broth into 6 chilled soup plates. Arrange the vegetables in the centre, top with a spoonful of fromage frais, garnish with the herbs and serve.

ROASTED WILD SCOTTISH SALMON WITH YOUNG SPINACH, GIROLLES & COURGETTE-FLOWER FRITTERS

For the fritter batter

200g plain flour
a pinch of salt
100ml olive oil
approximately 150ml water
2 egg whites

Sieve the flour and salt into a bowl and make a well in the centre. Mix the olive oil with the water and gradually stir this into the flour to make a smooth batter. It should resemble thick cream at this stage. Cover and leave to rest in a cool place for at least 2 hours.

For the courgette-flower fritters

6 small to medium-sized courgettes with flower attached,
    brushed of aphids, stalk end trimmed

Split the lower half of the courgette in two and leave the flower attached. Heat the deep-fat fryer to 190°C/375°F and fry the fritters when you're ready to assemble the dish.

For the salmon

We tend not to serve fish on the bone to our customers very often; rather I prefer to present a filleted piece of fish free of bones and sometimes skin also. However, I am adamant that *every* bone must be removed from the fish if it is to be served as a fillet, even if it means painstakingly pin-boning each one with tweezers.

90ml olive oil
6 x 150g pieces of salmon fillet, skin on and boned with tweezers
Maldon salt and pepper

Preheat the oven to 180°C/350°F/gas mark 4.

Heat the olive oil in a non-stick ovenproof pan and put in the fillets, flesh-side down. Heat until sealed and beginning to turn golden. Turn the fillets over to skin-side down, season with salt and pepper and place in the oven. Cook for 4–5 minutes depending on the thickness of the fillet. Test by piercing one in the thickest part with a sharp knife: if the flesh is still at all raw, return to the oven for a few more minutes. It should be moist and tender to the touch.

To serve

Whisk the whites for the batter until soft peaks are formed and fold them into the batter. Dip the courgettes into the batter one by one and fry them carefully in the hot oil until crisp and golden. Drain on 3 or 4 layers of kitchen paper and sprinkle with salt. Arrange them on 6 plates, placing the salmon on top, and the spinach and mushroom salad to one side.

SALAD OF YOUNG SPINACH LEAVES WITH GIROLLES

250g young spinach leaves, washed carefully and spun in a salad spinner
4 tbsp olive oil
1 clove garlic, crushed to a cream with salt
450g girolles or other wild mushrooms – left whole if small, or halved (I never use
*   shiitake mushrooms as I detest their smell, shape, texture and taste)*
salt and pepper
½ tsp chopped thyme leaves
1 tbsp chopped Italian flat-leaf parsley
½ tsp chopped chives

Place the spinach leaves in a large bowl. In a heavy-based frying pan heat the oil and garlic until sizzling, add the mushrooms and sauté over a high heat until they just begin to release their juices. Season and add the herbs. Pour the mushrooms and some of the juices into the salad bowl and toss gently with the spinach.

RASPBERRY & NECTARINE BRIOCHE
WITH RICH VANILLA CREAM

Making one's own brioche is a pleasure when it works but the dough can be difficult to handle and it is frustrating if it does not. This recipe is fairly foolproof but needs patience and preferably chilling overnight in the fridge to allow the butter to harden before rolling.

For the brioche

150g flour
25g sugar
a large pinch of salt
10g fresh yeast, creamed with warm water in a small cup until liquid
2 eggs, lightly whisked
100g butter at room temperature

Mix the dry ingredients together with the yeast in a mixing machine (not a food processor) or by hand until the yeast is evenly distributed. Add the eggs and mix to form a soft dough. Gradually beat in the butter little by little until completely amalgamated. It will be elastic, shiny and a little sticky. Cover the bowl with cling film and leave in a warm place to prove to double its volume, approximately 45 minutes.

Chill overnight.

For the fruit topping

4 ripe nectarines
caster sugar
500g raspberries
icing sugar

Divide the chilled dough into 6 equal pieces and shape roughly into balls. On a lightly floured surface, roll the dough into discs approximately 8cm across and place on a well-buttered baking sheet, allowing good spacing between each one. Cover with a piece of cling film and leave them in a warm draught-free place to rise to about half their size again. This may take up to 1 hour. Preheat the oven to 180°C/350°F/gas mark 4.

Cut the nectarines in half and remove the stones, slice into 3 or 4 wedges, depending on the size, and place in a bowl. Sprinkle with a little sugar. Divide the nectarine pieces between the brioches and arrange neatly on top, saving any juices which may be left in the bowl. Bake in the oven for 20–25 minutes or until the brioches are puffed and golden. Add the raspberries to the nectarine bowl with fruit syrup (if any) and toss gently together. Pile the raspberries on top of the nectarines and dust with a little icing sugar. Serve with Rich Vanilla Cream.

RICH VANILLA CREAM

125ml Crème anglaise (half the recipe on page 137)
200ml double cream, lightly whipped

Fold the whipped cream into the crème anglaise just before serving.

& SUMMER

Peach & Raspberry Champagne Cocktail

Melon & Ginger

Chilled Beetroot & Buttermilk Soup with Chives & Dill

Oven-Dried Tomato & Basil Pizza

Baked Red Pepper Filled with Tomato, Mozzarella & Basil

Finger Aubergines Baked with Herbed Crumbs

'Au Pactole' Carrots & Peas

Caesar Salad

'Bread Salad'

Shrimp & Courgette-Blossom Risotto

Crab, Avocado, Cucumber & Landcress Salad
with Dill & Maldon Salt Flat Bread

Summer Barbecue Menu: Hamburger, Guacamole
& Pickled Onions

Raspberry, Red Wine & Mint Sorbet

Zabaglione Cake with Strawberries

Almond Polenta Crumble Shortbread

'Summer Pudding'

Apricot & Bitter Kernel Jam

Redcurrant, Apple & Rosemary Jelly

PEACH & RASPBERRY
CHAMPAGNE COCKTAIL

2–3 very ripe peaches, quartered and stone removed
400g sweet soft raspberries, plus a few for decoration
20g caster sugar, optional
approximately 3 tbsp raspberry or peach liqueur, optional
1 bottle inexpensive Champagne or sparkling wine
ice cubes
6 sprigs of mint

Check that your food processor bowl and blade are scrupulously clean. Place the fruit in the bowl and purée until smooth. Taste and add a little sugar only if required. Push the purée through a small plastic or stainless-steel sieve into a small bowl. Add liqueur to taste if using and taste again. Place ice cubes in a glass jug and add half the Champagne or sparkling wine. Stir in the fruit purée gently, as the acid of the fruits will make the wine froth madly. To serve, pour the cocktail into tall glasses, half filling them. Top up with the remaining wine and decorate with the remaining raspberries and mint sprigs. For children this may be made with sparkling water or lemonade instead of Champagne.

MELON & GINGER

A perfectly ripe melon in the height of summer chosen from a market stall in any southern European town must be one of life's most delectable pleasures. Cut open, the luscious flesh can be scooped straight from its skin, without need of embellishment. Choose cantaloupe, cavaillon, galia, even the rather blowsy watermelon for a refreshing start or finish to a meal or as a cooling mid-afternoon 'reviver'.

This recipe combines the sweetness of the melon with the classic addition of ginger but thankfully not in its 1960s guest-house style — in powdered form.

150g fresh root ginger
250g caster sugar
450ml water
2 small ripe melons either the same or two different varieties
12 small mint leaves

Peel the ginger, slice it as fine as possible and then cut it into very fine strips, keeping the trimmings to one side. Place the fine strips in one small saucepan with half the sugar and water and the trimmings in another small saucepan with the remaining water and sugar. Place both on a very low heat and simmer until the liquids have reduced by half and the syrups have become golden in colour and the ginger is tender. This will take up to 20 minutes. Strain the ginger syrup from the trimmings pan into the shreds and allow to cool. Keep the cooked trimmings for another use, e.g. chopped and folded into lemon pudding or into a fruit cake.

Slice the top and bottom off each melon and then peel away the skin with a small sharp knife. Continue slicing around the melon in long large curved slices until the knife reaches the seeds, which should then be discarded. Place the slices in a serving bowl, scatter over the ginger shreds and pour in the syrup. Chill and serve garnished with mint.

CHILLED BEETROOT & BUTTERMILK SOUP WITH CHIVES & DILL

I learned to make this soup many years ago when sailing with friends around Corsica and Sardinia. It is a recipe which has Polish influences, notably from a dish called chlodnik, which also includes ingredients such as crayfish or shrimp, chopped hard-boiled egg and spring onion. This version has a shorter list of ingredients, thus making it simpler and lighter. The acidity of the buttermilk combined with the sweetness of the beetroot gives it an unusual flavour that is not to everyone's taste. One could even say it is an acquired taste! I have certainly acquired it, and find it both more-ish and refreshing in very hot weather.

750g cooked red beetroot, peeled
Maldon salt and pepper
2 tbsp finely chopped chives
1 tbsp finely chopped dill
1 litre buttermilk, whisked gently until smooth, or
    750ml milk mixed with 250ml soured cream
1 cucumber
1 bunch of spring onion, trimmed and washed well
a few ice cubes

Cut the beetroot into small dice and place them in a large bowl. Season with salt, pepper, chives and dill and toss together. Add the buttermilk or milk and cream mixture and stir until well mixed. Cover and chill in a refrigerator for up to 2 hours.

Cut the cucumber in half across, in half lengthwise and in half lengthwise again. Remove the seeds and cut each stick into three long sticks and then cut into dice. Slice the green and white parts of the spring onion finely and add to the soup with the cucumber dice. Add the ice cubes and stir. Serve in chilled soup bowls.

OVEN-DRIED TOMATO & BASIL PIZZA

500g ripe tomatoes, either cherry or plum
Maldon salt and pepper
90ml olive oil
1 tsp chopped thyme leaves
1 clove garlic, crushed to a cream with salt
4 large onions, peeled and finely sliced
1 bunch of basil, small tips reserved for garnish, larger leaves roughly chopped

PIZZA DOUGH
10g fresh yeast or 5g dried yeast
approximately 120ml warm water
200g strong plain flour
40ml olive oil
a pinch of salt
20ml milk

Preheat the oven to 150°C/300°F/gas mark 2.

Cut the cherry tomatoes in half or the plum tomatoes in sixths or eighths and place on a baking sheet, skin-side down. Sprinkle with salt and pepper. Cook in the oven for 1½ hours or until they have started to shrivel and dry.

To make the dough, mix the yeast and warm water until smooth and then add this to the remaining dough ingredients, either mixing and kneading by hand until smooth or using a mixing machine with the dough-hook attachment on the slowest speed. It will take 10–15 minutes for the dough to become smooth and soft to the touch. Place in a lightly oiled bowl, cover with cling film and leave to rise in a warm place for at least 1 hour.

Meanwhile, in a heavy-based pan heat the olive oil with the thyme and garlic until it begins to sizzle. Add the onions and stir over a high heat until they start to caramelize and turn golden. This may take up to 10 minutes. Season and turn the contents into a colander to drain and cool. Preheat the oven to 190°C/375°F/gas mark 5.

Remove the dough from the bowl and knead gently again until smooth. Roll the pizza dough to a disc approximately 25cm in diameter and place on a lightly oiled baking sheet. Spread the onions over it, leaving 2cm uncovered around the edge. With a fish slice or palette knife carefully dislodge the tomatoes from the tray and scatter them on top, skin-side down. Cover with cling film and leave in a warm draught-free place to rise for 15–20 minutes. The dough should look slightly risen and soft when ready to bake.

Place on the middle shelf. Bake for 15 minutes and sprinkle with the chopped basil. Return to the oven and bake for a further 5–10 minutes or until the crust is risen and golden. Slide on to a cooling rack if serving cold or serve straight from the oven garnished with basil sprigs.

BAKED RED PEPPER FILLED WITH TOMATO, MOZZARELLA & BASIL

Writing in *Italian Food*, Elizabeth David offers a very special recipe for the summer, Peperoni alla Piemontese. This recipe, possibly more than any other, has been borrowed, added to, adjusted and turned inside out by many a chef, and as a result is seen on many a menu in many a guise.

Clarke's is not alone in admitting that this is one of its many adaptations and that Mrs David is the source of inspiration behind it.

3 large red peppers
Maldon salt and pepper
3 beefsteak tomatoes or 6 smaller tomatoes, core removed with small knife
2 cloves garlic, peeled and sliced finely
6 tbsp olive oil
18 large basil leaves
4–6 balls buffalo mozzarella, sliced
6 sprigs basil

Preheat the oven to 180°C/350°F/gas mark 4.

Cut each pepper in half, including through the stalk. Remove the seeds carefully with a small sharp knife, allowing the stalk to remain in place. Season with salt and pepper. Dip the tomatoes into boiling water for 3–5 seconds, lift them into a bowl of iced water and remove the skin. Cut the tomatoes in half across the 'equator' line and gently squeeze out the seeds. Keep the skin and seeds for another use (e.g. Bloody Mary or Cracked Wheat Salad (pages 212 and 120), or in a tomato soup). Roughly chop the tomato and mix it in a bowl with the garlic, olive oil, salt, pepper and large basil leaves. Fill the pepper cavities with the tomato mixture and lay on a baking sheet or ovenproof dish.

Bake on the middle shelf of the oven for 30–40 minutes or until the peppers have started to collapse and are beginning to colour. When cool lift on to a serving platter and place slices of buffalo mozzarella on top with sprigs of basil.

FINGER AUBERGINES BAKED WITH HERBED CRUMBS

6 finger aubergines or 3 medium aubergines
90ml olive oil, plus a little extra for brushing
200g fresh breadcrumbs
2 cloves garlic, crushed to a cream with a little salt
2 tsp chopped thyme
1 tbsp chopped Italian flat-leaf parsley
salt and pepper

Preheat the oven to 190°C/375°F/gas mark 5.

Cut each aubergine in half lengthwise, including through the stalk. Gently slash the flesh with a sharp knife in a criss-cross fashion without cutting through to the skin. Brush with a little olive oil and char-grill (see grilling notes, page 170), or place under a salamander or bake in the preheated oven until tender and golden. Meanwhile heat the olive oil in a heavy-based pan and fry the breadcrumbs until golden and crisp. Remove from the heat and add the remaining ingredients.

Place the aubergine halves on a baking sheet cut side up. Carefully spoon the crumbs along the length and sprinkle with a little extra olive oil. Bake in the oven for 5–10 minutes or until sizzling and dark golden. Serve as an accompaniment to grilled meats or fish or as a light supper dish with shavings of Pecorino or Parmesan cheese and a green leaf and herb salad.

AU PACTOLE

Au Pactole was a wonderful restaurant on the Boulevard St-Germain in Paris. I worked there in the mid-1970s for three months, as an unpaid *commis*. Although my time there was short I was able to observe, first-hand, its chef-patron, the late Jacques Manière, create dishes that were true examples of the then recently born 'nouvelle cuisine'. In fact he was one of the original exponents of the movement, along with such eminent chefs as Alain Chapel, Jean and Pierre Troisgros and Michel Guèrard. Together, they encouraged shorter cooking times and lighter approaches to the creation of sauces, and generally simplified the heaviness and richness that had become synonymous with French cooking. This brought about a new concept of eating in France. However, by the mid-1980s this style of cooking had acquired a bad name. Nouvelle cuisine had become for many young cooks an excuse to serve minuscule portions of experimental and usually inappropriate combinations of flavours on one plate. Too many inexperienced chefs tried to mimic their masters without sufficient knowledge of why and how the ideas had evolved, thus destroying the name of nouvelle cuisine and putting it into disrepute.

Although I was fortunate enough to witness Jacques Manière create this particular dish almost every day to serve either with roasted squab pigeon or roasted new season lamb, I always felt that it was delicious enough to be eaten directly from the pan! For me it is the essence of what nouvelle cuisine was about. Well-prepared ingredients, cooked in as short a time as possible, with only as much fuss and fiddle as necessary to produce an uncomplicated dish which tasted as fresh cooked as it did raw.

'AU PACTOLE' CARROTS & PEAS

50g unsalted butter, cut into small cubes
600g young carrots, scrubbed and sliced finely on the angle
Maldon salt and pepper
350g small podded peas (approximately 1.2 kg unpodded)
2 tbsp chopped tarragon leaves

Only use freshly podded peas and young carrots. Choose a pan only a little larger than is necessary to hold all the ingredients at once. Put the butter in first. Add the carrots and a little salt and pepper and cover with water (approximately 150ml). Add the peas, a little more seasoning and then the tarragon. Cover with a small circular piece of greaseproof paper and then the lid. Place on a high heat and cook until all but a drop of the water has evaporated and the peas are cooked. Toss the vegetables together and serve immediately.

CAESAR SALAD

¼ baguette, cut into 1cm cubes
1 tsp chopped thyme
30ml olive oil
2 cloves garlic, crushed to a cream
salt and pepper
1 egg
½ tbsp Dijon mustard
150ml olive oil
salt and pepper
juice of 1 lemon
2 small cos lettuces
a few leaves of Italian flat-leaf parsley
150g Parmesan, finely shaved with vegetable peeler
6 salted anchovies, rinsed and filleted, or 12 anchovy fillets in oil

Preheat the oven to 150°C/300°F/gas mark 2.

Toss the bread cubes in a bowl with the thyme, olive oil, garlic, salt and pepper. Spread over a baking sheet and bake for up to 20 minutes or until golden and crisp.

Whisk the egg with the mustard until blended. Continue whisking whilst pouring in the oil very slowly until the dressing has emulsified. Add salt and pepper and the lemon juice then a drop of water to loosen the consistency. It should be like double cream.

Prepare the cos lettuce by removing the outside leaves and washing the heart leaves gently. Spin them in a salad spinner. To serve, break the larger leaves into half and place with the smaller leaves and parsley leaves in a bowl with a drizzle of the dressing. Toss gently together and arrange on individual salad plates, placing the toasted cubes, Parmesan and anchovies in and amongst the leaves attractively. Drizzle a little extra dressing around the salad. Alternatively, arrange the salad in a similar way in a large salad bowl to serve at the table.

'BREAD SALAD'

Traditionally this dish is made in Tuscany with stale bread which has been soaked in water, squeezed out and tossed with various ingredients. Here, most of the traditional ingredients are used, but they are assembled in a different way using both wild rocket, with its long heavily indented leaves, and garden rocket, which has a rounder softer shape. Both have a wonderful peppery taste.

1 ficelle (fine baguette), or a quarter baguette
2 cloves garlic, crushed to a cream with salt
60ml good olive oil
Maldon salt and pepper
zest and juice of 1 lemon
6 large ripe tomatoes
half a cucumber
200g olive-oil-marinated black olives, pitted and halved
6 salted anchovy fillets, roughly chopped
a handful of flat-leaved parsley leaves
150g mixed wild and garden rocket leaves
6 lemon wedges

Cut the ficelle into thin slices at an angle or the baguette into walnut-sized cubes and place in a bowl with half the garlic, a drizzle of olive oil, salt, pepper and the lemon zest. Toss together and leave to marinate for a few minutes.

Blanch the tomatoes in boiling water for 2–3 seconds, dip into iced water and peel. Cut into quarters and remove the seeds, then core and cut each piece into halves. (Keep this debris with the skin for another use, e.g. Bloody Mary, Cracked Wheat Salad or Soup of Five Tomatoes and Three Beetroots, pages 212, 120 and 113.) Season the tomatoes in a small bowl with the remaining garlic, salt, pepper, the lemon juice and a little olive oil.

Cut the cucumber into four lengthwise and remove the seeds with a sharp knife. Cut each stick in half again lengthwise and then at an angle into small diamond shapes and toss into the tomato with the olives, anchovies, parsley and marinated bread. Cover and leave to chill in a refrigerator for up to 1 hour.

To serve, toss the rocket leaves together with a drizzle of olive oil, and salt and pepper. Arrange the leaves on 6 chilled salad plates and pile the bread and tomato mixture over the top attractively. Spin a fine stream of olive oil over the salad and garnish with a lemon wedge.

SHRIMP & COURGETTE-BLOSSOM RISOTTO

3 tbsp good olive oil
125g butter, at room temperature
2 medium onions, finely diced
350g Arborio or Carnaroli rice
250ml dry white wine
800ml Vegetable or Fish Stock (page 38), warm
250g courgette, cut into small dice
salt and pepper
600g shrimp, cooked, in the shell or 300g shrimp, cooked and peeled
6 courgette blossoms, chopped
1 tsp chopped tarragon

In a heavy-based pan warm the olive oil with 75g butter until melted. Over a gentle heat stir in the onion and cook until transparent. Add the rice and continue to cook until the grains of rice are thoroughly coated in the oil. Turn up the heat a little and stir in the wine. When the wine has almost completely evaporated, gradually start adding the broth, a ladleful at a time, stirring continuously to prevent the rice catching on the base of the pan, and allowing the rice to absorb the liquid before adding the next ladle. This will take 12–15 minutes, during which time the grains will start to soften and the liquid will begin to take on a creamy consistency. Halfway through the cooking add the dice of courgette and salt and pepper and stir well into the rice.

From time to time test a grain of rice by biting into it. If the centre is still at all raw, continue to cook gently. The rice should retain a very slight bite but if it is left too al dente it will be indigestible. As soon as the rice is cooked remove it from the heat. Immediately stir in the shrimps, courgette blossom and finally the remaining butter and tarragon. Taste for seasoning and serve.

CRAB, AVOCADO, CUCUMBER & LANDCRESS SALAD WITH DILL & MALDON SALT FLAT BREAD

If I was told that I had one meal left in my life and that I had to choose the menu, it would without any doubt have to include crab. Fresh, unadulterated, chilled, lightly seasoned, fabulous crab is one of my most favourite foods. We are so lucky in having a supplier in the West Country who catches, cooks, picks and delivers the crab to us, all within twenty-four hours. If it were not so expensive I would even consider placing it on the menu every day that he could supply us! There is no point in making this recipe unless your fishmonger can guarantee to you a crab of absolute freshness.

Dill & Maldon Salt Flat Bread

The flavour of this flat bread can easily be adapted by adding a different herb to the basic dough. Once we added very finely chopped chili instead of a herb, which produced a wonderfully spicy bread.

150g strong flour
a pinch of salt
5g fresh yeast or a pinch of dried yeast
30ml olive oil, plus a little for brushing
about 70ml warm water
1 tbsp chopped dill
½ tbsp Maldon salt

Preheat the oven to 180°C/350°F/gas mark 4.

Sieve the flour and salt into a mixing bowl. Mix the yeast, olive oil and warm water until smooth and pour into the flour, mixing gently to form a ball. Turn out on to a lightly floured board and knead until smooth, approximately

10 minutes. This could be mixed in a mixing machine with the dough-hook attachment. Place into a lightly oiled bowl, cover and leave in a warm but not hot place until it has doubled its bulk. Knead again until smooth, adding the dill, and break into walnut-sized pieces. Ideally this bread should be rolled very thinly before baking. Brush two baking sheets with olive oil.

Normally we use the pasta-rolling machine for this but, with a lot of elbow grease, a rolling pin will do just fine. Roll very thinly into long narrow sheets approximately 10 cm x 30 cm and place on the baking sheets, one at a time. Sprinkle with Maldon salt and bake in oven for 10–12 minutes or until golden and crisp. Remove carefully from the tray and cool. Break into rough shapes to serve.

For the dressing

1 egg
150ml olive oil
salt and pepper
juice of 1 lemon
75g brown crab meat, sieved

To make the dressing, whisk the egg until frothy and very gradually add the olive oil until an emulsion is formed. It should have the consistency of double cream. Season with salt and pepper, add the lemon juice and stir in the brown crab meat. Cover and keep refrigerated.

For the salad

½ cucumber
2 avocados
juice of 2 lemons
300g white crab meat
1 tbsp chopped chervil
1 tbsp chopped dill
1 tbsp chopped chives
6 lemon wedges
150g landcress or other small salad leaves

Cut the cucumber in half and scoop out the seeds. Cut each cucumber half into thick strips, then cut across into small dice. Cut the avocados into halves and brush with a little of the lemon juice. Keep both refrigerated.

Check through the white crab meat and remove any stray pieces of shell. Place in a bowl with the herbs, remaining lemon juice, salt and pepper. Mix gently together, cover and leave in the refrigerator.

To serve, place the salad leaves in a bowl, drizzle with a little olive oil, season with salt and pepper and toss gently. Add the cucumber to the white crab salad, tossing gently. Cut each avocado half lengthwise into 6 slices. Place 1 piece of flat bread on each plate and arrange the leaves on top. Scatter the crab and cucumber over and arrange with avocado slices neatly. Pour a little crab dressing on and around the salad and serve the rest separately. Garnish with the lemon wedges.

GRILLING

Many of the recipes contained in this book require a char grill or barbecue to cook the ingredients. Quite obviously these are not items of equipment found in every home, but for most recipes a griddle pan, a salamander (overhead grill) or the grill inside an oven, if preheated for long enough, are ideal alternatives. If a barbecue can be set up in the garden the grilling results are even more pleasing as the heat created with real charcoal or briquettes is far more intense than that of an electric or gas grill.

If using a grill with iron bars it is important to sear the outside of the food first over the most intense source of heat. Once the outside has started to caramelize and colour, the food must be turned 90° to create the criss-cross markings. As soon as the required amount of colouring has been achieved, the food must be turned over and moved to a cooler part of the grill, if a more gentle cooking is needed, as for most meats. For vegetables, such as fennel, courgette or aubergine, a good high heat throughout is preferable. If using a salamander, the food needs to be first placed on a metal baking sheet or metal tray which will assist in conducting the heat from below the food. It is most important that the heat source is preheated for at least 10–15 minutes before using. If using a griddle pan, wipe with vegetable oil before heating and then drizzle with olive oil just before laying the food on to the pan for cooking.

Summer Barbecue Menu: Hamburger, Guacamole & Pickled Onions

Hamburger

1.2 kg lean grass-fed beef
100g beef fat
Maldon salt
1 chili, finely chopped, including seeds
1 tbsp roughly chopped parsley
1 tbsp roughly chopped coriander
1 tsp chopped thyme
1 tbsp Dijon mustard
1 tsp lemon zest

Cut the meat and fat into large cubes and grind through a small to medium aperture on the mincing attachment of a mixing machine, pushing the fat through last. Alternatively ask your butcher to do this for you. Place all the ingredients in a large bowl and mix thoroughly making sure that the fat and other ingredients are evenly distributed throughout the meat. Divide the mixture into six and shape using cupped hands into round patties approximately 2½cm high, making sure that the meat is firmly but not rigidly pressed together. Heat a grill or griddle pan to its highest heat and grill until dark bar marks appear. Criss-cross by turning the hamburger 90° and continue to cook. Turn over and repeat the process until cooked as required. For medium rare this will take 4–6 minutes in total. Test the hamburger by pressing gently on the top: the outside should be crusty and charred and the juices which flow out should be reddish brown. Serve immediately with soft sesame seed rolls and Heinz Tomato Ketchup or the following Guacamole.

GUACAMOLE

There are countless incorrect recipes for this classic South American dish but there is one way only to make it properly, by simply using the correct ingredients with *no additions*! No garlic, no tomatoes, no olive oil, no black pepper, *just* —

3 ripe avocados, peeled and blemishes removed
juice of 3 large limes
1—2 small red chilies, very finely chopped, with seeds
salt
2 tbsp roughly chopped coriander leaves

With a fork, mash the avocados in a bowl until almost smooth — a few lumps are fine. Stir in the lime juice and add the chilies and salt. Cover with cling film and chill for up to 1 hour. Stir in the coriander and adjust to taste by adding more chilies, lime juice or salt.

As well as the relish for grilled hamburger, guacamole is also excellent served with grilled rump steak or barbecued chicken, and as a snack with deep-fried tortilla chips.

PICKLED ONIONS

For 4 x ½ litre jars

1.2 kg pickling onions
1.2 litres white wine vinegar
1 litre dry white wine
2 tsp mustard seeds
2 red chilies, each sliced into 4 lengthwise
8 bay leaves
8 sprigs of rosemary
2 tsp salt

Preheat the oven to 180°C/350°F/gas mark 4.

Bring a pan of water to the boil and tip in all the onions. Boil for a few seconds, drain and cool. With a small knife peel the skins away from the onions and trim the root end carefully. Some shops now stock ready peeled pickling onions, which will save a lot of time! Meanwhile lay the 4 scrupulously clean jars on a baking sheet and sterilize in the oven for 10 minutes and boil the lids in a small pan of water for 5 minutes to sterilize.

Bring the remaining ingredients to the boil. Fill the pots immediately with the onions and divide the herbs and chili pieces evenly between them. Pour the hot liquid over, screw the lids on firmly and cool. Store in a cool dark place for at least 4 weeks before serving. Unopened they will keep for up to 6 months.

Raspberry, Red Wine & Mint Sorbet

500g raspberries
400ml light red wine (Beaujolais or Sancerre or Valpolicella)
100g sugar
25g mint leaves, plus 6 sprigs

Heat all the ingredients except the mint sprigs together in a stainless-steel pan and simmer for 5–10 minutes. Strain through a sieve and discard the debris. Cool the liquid and churn in an ice-cream machine or freeze in a freezer tray and scrape the ice crystals as they form from time to time. Serve within 12 hours, decorated with the mint sprigs.

APRICOT & BITTER KERNEL JAM

Makes 1.75 kg

1.25 kg ripe apricots
800 g granulated sugar
juice of 3 lemons

Wash the apricots, cut them in half and remove the stones but retain them. Place the apricots in a deep bowl, layering with the sugar, and leave covered overnight to macerate. Crack the stones carefully and remove the bitter kernels. Blanch them in boiling water for 2 minutes, rub away the skins and slice the kernels into slivers.

The following day place the sugared fruit in a large heavy pan with the lemon juice and bring to a simmer over a gentle heat. Turn up the heat and boil gently, skimming occasionally, until the setting point is achieved. The best way to check the setting point is by placing a saucer in a refrigerator while the jam is boiling. Every so often drop 1 tsp of the jam on to the saucer and return to the fridge. After a few seconds the jam should look slightly wrinkled as the saucer is tipped to one side. This will result in a semi-set jam, which I feel is best for a summer fruit.

Meanwhile preheat the oven to 180°C/350°F/gas mark 4. Lay the 6 scrupulously clean jam jars on a baking sheet and sterilize in the oven for 10 minutes. Boil the lids in a small pan of water for 5 minutes to sterilize. Stir the kernels into the jam and fill the pots immediately, screwing the lids on firmly.

Redcurrant, Apple & Rosemary Jelly

Makes 5 x 200 ml jars

1 kg Bramley apples, washed and left whole
750 g redcurrants, picked off the stems, washed gently
25 g fresh rosemary on sprays, plus 5 small sprigs for the jars
approximately 1.25 litres water
approximately 650 g granulated sugar
juice of 2 lemons

Chop the apples, including cores, and place all the fruit in a large heavy pan with the rosemary and just cover with water. Simmer gently until the fruit is soft, approximately 30 minutes. Strain through a jelly bag overnight.

The following day preheat the oven to 180°C/350°F/gas mark 4. Weigh the juice – it will be around 1.3 kg – and measure half that amount in sugar. Over a low heat dissolve the sugar with the fruit juice and lemon juice. Bring to a gentle boil and cook until the setting point is reached, skimming very carefully when necessary. The best way to check the setting point is by placing a saucer in a refrigerator while the jelly is boiling. Every so often drop 1 tsp of the jelly on to the saucer and return to the fridge. After a few seconds the jelly should look slightly wrinkled as the saucer is tipped to one side.

Meanwhile sterilize the jam jars and lids. Lay the 6 scrupulously clean jam jars on a baking sheet and sterilize in the oven for 10 minutes and boil the lids in a small pan of water for 5 minutes. In a separate pan of water boil the remaining sprigs of rosemary to sterilize them, and place these in the jars. Fill with the jelly, cover tightly with the lids and allow to cool and set. This jelly should be stored in a cool dark place and will keep for up to 1 year.

AUTUMN

LUNCH

Roasted Gem Squash with Ceps, Cream,
Rosemary & White Truffle

Mousse of Duck Liver with Cobnut, Celery
& Landcress Salad; Walnut Toasts

Stilton Cheese with Apples, Pears,
Suffolk Grapes & Figs

ROASTED GEM SQUASH WITH CEPS, CREAM, ROSEMARY & WHITE TRUFFLE

6 gem squash, the size of tennis balls
100ml olive oil, plus a little extra for frying
3 cloves garlic, crushed to a cream with salt
salt and pepper
2 tsp chopped rosemary leaves
300ml double cream
500g fresh ceps, brushed of sand and sliced, or other wild mushrooms,
    or brown cap field mushrooms
1 tbsp chopped parsley
approximately 30g white truffle (optional)
6 sprigs of rosemary and 6 sprigs of parsley

Preheat the oven to 180°C/350°F/gas mark 4.

Scrub the gem squash thoroughly and cook in pan of boiling salted water for 3–5 minutes, depending on their size. They should not crack or burst open. Remove and allow to cool naturally. With a firm sharp knife, slice off the top quarter and retain it, scoop out the seeds and discard them, and place the squash on a baking sheet. Mix the olive oil, a third of the garlic, salt, pepper and half the rosemary together, spoon this into the cavities and replace the tops. Roast for 30–35 minutes or until the flesh has softened. Meanwhile, simmer the cream with half the remaining garlic and the remaining rosemary on a very low heat. Season to taste. In a heavy-based frying pan, heat a drizzle of olive oil and the remaining garlic until sizzling and add the mushrooms. Toss over a high heat until golden, season and add the parsley.

To serve place the gem squash in 6 soup bowls and divide the cream between them. Scoop the mushrooms on top, shave truffle over the mushrooms if using, and garnish with rosemary and parsley sprigs, the 'lid' decoratively leaning on one side of the squash.

MOUSSE OF DUCK LIVER WITH COBNUT, CELERY & LANDCRESS SALAD; WALNUT TOASTS

900g fresh duck livers, trimmed of all green-tinged parts and sinew
75g unsalted butter
2 shallots, peeled and finely sliced
2 tsp chopped thyme leaves
2 cloves garlic, crushed to a cream with salt
salt and pepper
1 tbsp honey
1 tbsp armagnac or cognac (optional)

Rinse the livers in cold water and drain well.

Melt the butter in a heavy-based pan but do not brown it. Add the shallots and cook them gently until soft. Add the thyme, garlic and livers and continue to cook gently, stirring occasionally until the livers have turned pale brown and have become a little firm. They should remain slightly pink inside. Season and stir in the honey, and armagnac or cognac if using. Pour the contents of the pan into a liquidizer or food processor and purée until very smooth. Taste for seasoning and pour into a shallow dish to cool. Cover well with cling film and serve from the refrigerator. Eat within 2–3 days.

COBNUT, CELERY & LANDCRESS SALAD

500g cobnuts (unshelled weight) or 150g shelled hazelnuts or walnuts
olive oil
salt and pepper
100g landcress
2 celery hearts

Preheat the oven to 180°C/350°F/gas mark 4. Crack the cobnuts carefully and place them, or the hazelnuts or walnuts if using, on a baking sheet. Do not worry if a few are broken or crushed. Drizzle with a little olive oil, salt and pepper and roast for up to 30 minutes or until crisp and golden. Allow to cool. Meanwhile pick the long stalks away from the landcress and rinse in cold water. Spin gently in a salad spinner and place in a bowl. Trim the celery to expose the tender yellow stalk and leaves and cut into even lengths, approximately 5–6cm. Rinse and spin as before. Add the nuts to the salad, drizzle with olive oil, salt and pepper and toss gently. Arrange on individual plates or in a salad bowl.

WALNUT BREAD

240g wholewheat flour, plus a little for sprinkling
260g strong white flour, plus a little for dusting
5g salt
15g fresh yeast or 7g dried yeast
250ml warm water
50ml walnut oil, plus a little for brushing
125g walnut halves, very roughly chopped

In a mixing bowl mix the flours with the salt. In a small bowl mix the yeast with half the warm water and using the dough-hook attachment on the slowest speed pour this into the mixing bowl. Add the walnut oil and then most of the remaining warm water to produce a soft dough. Continue to knead until the dough becomes smooth, approximately 5–8 minutes, adding the remaining water if necessary. Alternatively the mixing can be done by hand in a medium-sized bowl and then turned out on to a clean table and kneaded for 5–10 minutes until smooth. Place the dough in a clean bowl which has a light coating of walnut oil. Cover with cling film and leave in a warm place to rise to double its size. This may take up to 1 hour depending on the temperature of the kitchen and the weather.

Preheat the oven to 180°C/350°F/gas mark 4. Sprinkle a baking sheet with a little wholewheat flour. Remove the dough from the bowl and place on a table lightly dusted with white flour. Sprinkle the walnuts on top and gently knead them in until they are evenly distributed, expelling the air in the dough at the same time. Cut in two and shape the loaves into round balls or long sausage shapes and place on the baking sheet. Brush with a little walnut oil, cover with cling film and allow to rise in a warm place to half the size again. Place on the middle shelf of the oven and turn up the temperature to 205°C/400°F/gas mark 6. Bake until crisp and dark golden brown. This may take up to 40–45 minutes, by which time the bread will sound hollow when the base is knocked. Cool and use within 2 days.

WALNUT BREAD TOASTS

¼ walnut loaf, preferably 1–2 days old
15ml walnut oil or olive oil

Preheat the oven to 160°C/325°F/gas mark 3.

Slice the walnut bread as thinly as possible with a serrated knife, approximately 3 slices per person. Lay on a baking sheet, slightly overlapping, and drizzle with walnut or olive oil.

Bake for 12–15 minutes or until crisp and curled. Turn over and bake again for a few minutes. These are best eaten within a few hours but will keep for a few days in a sealed container.

Stilton Cheese with Apples, Pears, Suffolk Grapes & Figs

The tiny Nottinghamshire village of Colston Bassett is famous for one of Britain's best-known cheeses. This Stilton is the most creamy in texture and the most succulent of them all and at & Clarke's we sell over 300 kg each year. The quality of each cheese can easily be judged by assessing the quantity of the creamy-white content compared to the blue in its interior, which should be the smaller. The more mature the cheese, the creamier the texture will be.

Stilton is a very popular cheese to serve at Christmas and the New Year, but in the cooler autumn months it can also be a satisfying way to end a meal. Either whole or halved, wrapped in a linen napkin or tea towel, it looks both majestic and enticing. Thankfully, gone are the days when it was thought clever to scoop out the creamy blue centre first and fill the cavity with port wine: clearly a waste of the good cheese *and* the port. Now most people are aware that the best way to make the most of a Stilton, and to make it last as long as possible, is to 'carve' the cheese. Holding the knife horizontally, parallel with the cut surface of the cheese; the point of the knife should be towards the centre and the heel of the knife at the crust's edge. With gentle slicing movements at a slight downward angle, pieces of the cheese can be cut, with equal amounts of the blue and the white parts as well as the crusty rind.

Because of its sharp and salty flavour, a good plain oatmeal biscuit (page 83) or a water biscuit is its perfect accompaniment.

I enjoy eating fresh fruits with Stilton as I find them to be not only palate cleansing but also a good balance to its richness. The big fat figs which we buy in the autumn from a friend in Suffolk are ripened on a south-facing wall. To serve them, they are simply rinsed, their knobbly tips trimmed and the fruit is then split in half to reveal the luscious juicy flesh. With these figs we often serve small clusters of grapes which have been grown in the same walled garden. Plainly arranged on the fig and grape leaves, they are served with organically grown apples and pears from Brogdale Farm in Kent.

SUPPER

Thyme & Maldon Salt Breadsticks

Salad of Buffalo Mozzarella with Grapes,
Capers & Olives

Roasted Free-Range Chicken with Crostini of
Wild Mushrooms, Pancetta & Watercress Leaves

Spiced Apple & Prune Strudel

THYME & MALDON SALT
BREADSTICKS

Makes 24 breadsticks

300g flour
½ tsp salt
approximately 180ml warm water
10g yeast or 5g dried yeast
60ml olive oil, plus a little for brushing
2 tsp chopped thyme
Maldon salt

In a mixing bowl mix the flour and salt. In a small bowl mix half the water with the yeast and olive oil until the yeast is smooth. Pour this into the flour and mix on a slow speed with the dough-hook attachment until the dough is smooth, adding the remaining water when necessary. Alternatively the mixing can be done by hand in a medium-sized bowl and then turned out on to a clean table and kneaded for 5–10 minutes until smooth. Place the dough in a clean bowl and cover with cling film and leave in a warm place for up to 1 hour or until it has doubled in bulk. Preheat the oven to 180°C/350°F/gas mark 4.

Turn the dough out on to a board, sprinkle with the thyme and knead to expel the excess air. Cut the dough into 24 walnut-sized pieces. One at a time, roll them by hand into long thin sticks, placing them on to a well-oiled baking sheet, not touching each other. Gently brush the sticks with olive oil and sprinkle with Maldon salt. Allow to prove for 5–10 minutes in a warm, draught-free place and then bake for 12–15 minutes until crisp and golden.

SALAD OF BUFFALO MOZZARELLA WITH GRAPES, CAPERS & OLIVES

I have many, many happy memories of meals with Alice Waters, either at her home in California or at her restaurant, Chez Panisse; on each occasion I have come away enriched. I have perhaps learnt a different way of presenting a certain dish or been able to taste an unfamiliar ingredient or been introduced to a fascinating and accomplished friend involved in wine making or in growing something wonderful. One of Alice's many appealing characteristics is her love and admiration of her friends. She is constantly praising and encouraging. She told me one evening that one of her friends, living in the South of France, had once prepared for her a memorable salad which was quite interesting in its diversity of ingredients.

This friend had combined a long list of ingredients including grapes, salted anchovy, chili, capers and olives with garlic and leaves of coriander. It sounded enticing to me as I enjoy all these ingredients singularly but I was curious to know how they combined. So immediately on my return to London I decided to experiment with this combination. I loved the flavours and as a result the following salad has had a firm place on both our lunch and dinner menus.

300g marinated black olives, halved and stones removed
1 tbsp baby capers, drained
2 tbsp balsamic vinegar
1 clove garlic, crushed to a cream with a little salt
1 small red chili, very finely chopped, including seeds
60ml olive oil
Maldon salt
350g purple grapes, washed, halved and deseeded
350g green grapes, washed, halved and deseeded
1 small red onion, peeled, halved and sliced fine
a few parsley and coriander leaves
6 balls of buffalo mozzarella
pepper
good olive oil

Mix the olives and capers with the balsamic vinegar, garlic, chili, olive oil and salt and toss gently. Leave to marinate for at least 30 minutes. To serve add the grapes, onion and herbs and toss together. Arrange neatly on 6 serving plates. Slice or wedge the mozzarella and season with salt and pepper and place on top of the salad. Drizzle with good olive oil.

For an interesting variation to this recipe, chop 6 salted anchovy fillets and add to the olive and caper marinade.

Serve with Thyme & Maldon Salt Breadsticks (page 192).

ROASTED FREE-RANGE CHICKEN WITH CROSTINI OF WILD MUSHROOMS, PANCETTA & WATERCRESS LEAVES

This recipe will serve 6 very hungry people or 8 with normal appetites

2 x 1.5kg free-range chickens
salt and pepper
3 tbsp chopped thyme leaves
1 lemon, quartered
2 large onions, peeled and chopped roughly
3 large carrots, peeled and chopped roughly
4 stalks celery, chopped roughly
1 head fennel, chopped roughly
90ml olive oil, plus more for drizzling
1 head garlic, chopped in small pieces
½ bottle hearty red wine
500ml Light or Dark Chicken Stock or Vegetable Stock (pages 39, 40 and 37)

Preheat the oven to 180°C/350°F/gas mark 4.

Trim the chickens of excess fat, the parson's nose and the skin from the neck ends, and remove any string which may be holding the legs against the breasts. Sprinkle the cavities with salt, pepper, and 1 tbsp of the thyme. Add the lemon pieces. In a heavy-based roasting tin place the vegetables, olive oil and garlic and heat on a medium heat on the stove top. Stir the vegetables from time to time as they cook and when they begin to brown put the chickens, breast sides down, on top of the bed of vegetables. Season with salt, pepper and half the remaining thyme and drizzle with olive oil. Roast in the preheated oven for 20 minutes. Remove the roasting tin from the oven, turn the chickens over and season again as before. Scrape the vegetables which may have stuck to the base of the tin to dislodge them. Return the chickens to the oven, turn down temperature to 160°C/325°F/gas mark 3 and continue to roast for a further 40 minutes or until the thigh juices run clear when pierced with a skewer.

Remove the chickens to a dish and cover with an upturned bowl. Skim any excess fat away from the roasting tin and discard. Place the tin on the stove on a medium heat. Add the red wine to the pan, and cook until the wine has all but evaporated. Add the chicken or vegetable stock and bring to the boil, scraping the vegetables away from the bottom of the tin as this will give colour to the sauce. Simmer and season to taste. Strain into a small pan and skim if necessary.

To carve the chicken, first remove the legs, inserting the knife firmly into the indentation between the breast and thigh. Cut the leg in two at the joint of the thigh and drumstick. Trim away and discard the knuckle of the drumstick. Next remove the breasts from the carcass and cut each into two at a slight angle.

Serve with the wild mushroom and pancetta crostini and the watercress salad, pouring a little of the sauce around each portion and serving the rest separately.

WILD MUSHROOM & PANCETTA CROSTINI

500g wild mushrooms
6 slices good bread
3 tbsp olive oil, plus extra for drizzling
salt and pepper
2 cloves garlic, crushed to a cream with salt
12 slices pancetta
1 tbsp chopped thyme
Maldon salt
3 bunches of watercress, washed, thick stalks removed and spun in salad spinner

Brush the mushrooms and break them carefully into even-sized pieces. Drizzle the bread with olive oil, season with salt and pepper and scrape with a touch of the garlic paste. In a heavy-based non-stick frying pan, heat a drop of olive oil and fry the pancetta on both sides until crisp. Keeping the fat in the pan, remove the pancetta to kitchen paper and keep warm. If using a char grill, grill the bread on both sides until golden and keep warm. Alternatively use a salamander for this. Add the remaining oil to the frying pan, heat it and fry the mushrooms with the thyme, salt, pepper and the remaining garlic until the juices just start to be released.

Just before serving, place the watercress leaves in a salad bowl with a drizzle of olive oil, Maldon salt and pepper. Toss them gently and serve to one side of the roasted chicken with the mushrooms and pancetta piled on top of the crostini.

SPICED APPLE & PRUNE STRUDEL

900g Bramley apples
300g eating apples, such as Cox's, Jonagold or Spartan
12 pitted prunes, soaked overnight in the juice of 2 oranges
zest of 1 lemon
zest of 1 orange
150g sultanas or raisins
75g Demerara sugar or 2 tbsp runny honey
2 tsp mixed spice
a pinch of ground black pepper
6 sheets of frozen or fresh filo pastry
50g butter, melted

TO SERVE
250ml double cream, whipped

Peel and core all the apples and cut them into walnut-sized pieces. Place them in a bowl with all the remaining ingredients except the filo pastry and butter. Toss gently together and leave on one side.

Preheat the oven to 190°C/375°F/gas mark 5. Unroll the filo pastry and check that all sheets are unbroken. Cover with a cloth to prevent them from drying. Brush a baking sheet with a little of the butter.

Lay a clean tea towel short side towards you on the work surface and lay a sheet of pastry on top, long side towards you. Brush with a little butter and place the next sheet on top of half the first sheet, increasing the depth. Brush again with butter. Place the third sheet over the area covered by the first sheet and continue layering and buttering as before. Using a slotted spoon, pile the fruit along the length of the front edge making sure that the prunes are evenly distributed. Lift the front edge of the tea towel up gently, and carefully but firmly begin to roll the pastry around the apple into a sausage shape, tucking in the ends to prevent the apple from falling out.

Just before reaching the far end, brush the final 2 cm of filo pastry with butter and press the roll over this to seal it well. With the aid of the tea towel lift the strudel on to the baking sheet and bake for approximately 30 minutes or until crisp and golden. Serve warm or chilled the following day with lots of whipped cream.

DINNER

Salad of Rare Roasted Beef Fillet with Salted Anchovies,
Parmesan & Capers; Parmesan Toasts

Grilled Turbot, Marinated Peppers, Olives & Parsley
with Potato-Chive Pancake

Appleby Cheshire Cheese with Fresh Walnuts

Poached Autumn Fruits in Marsala & Spices

SALAD OF RARE ROASTED BEEF FILLET WITH SALTED ANCHOVIES, PARMESAN & CAPERS; PARMESAN TOASTS

30ml olive oil, plus a little extra for drizzling
freshly ground black pepper
750g piece of grass-fed beef fillet, trimmed of excess fat and sinew
salt
12 salted anchovies
1 tsp chopped thyme
150g selection of salad leaves, for example rocket, landcress, watercress
150g Parmesan in one piece, shaved with a sharp knife or vegetable peeler
     into fine wafers
a few capers, drained
good olive oil
6 lemon wedges

Rub the olive oil and pepper all over the beef fillet and leave it on a plate to marinate in a cool place, covered, for up to 1 hour. Preheat the oven to 200°C/400°F/gas mark 6.

In a heavy-based ovenproof pan or roasting tin, heat a drizzle of olive oil until smoking, add the fillet and turn the meat constantly to seal the outside, approximately 4–5 minutes. Sprinkle with a little salt and roast in the oven for 5 minutes for a medium-rare result. Test by inserting a metal skewer into the centre of the meat: the tip should still feel cold to the touch when removed. Remove the fillet from the pan and allow to cool.

To prepare the anchovies, rinse under cold running water, gently removing the fillets from the backbones. Discard the bones and innards. Place the fillets flesh side up on a plate and sprinkle with thyme and olive oil. Cover and leave in a cool place.

To serve, place the salad leaves in a bowl, drizzle olive oil over them and add

salt and pepper. Toss gently and arrange on one side of 6 salad plates. Slice the beef thinly with a sharp knife and place 2 or 3 slices on the opposite side. Arrange the Parmesan shavings and anchovy fillets attractively over the top of the meat, sprinkle with capers and drizzle with a little good olive oil. Garnish with lemon wedges and serve with the Parmesan Toasts.

PARMESAN BREAD

500g strong white flour, plus a little for sprinkling
100g grated Parmesan
5g salt
15g yeast or 10g dried yeast
200ml warm water
50ml olive oil, plus a little for brushing
2 eggs, lightly whisked

In a mixing bowl mix the flour, Parmesan and salt. In a small bowl mix the yeast with half the warm water until smooth. Add this with the olive oil and most of the egg to the flour and mix on the slowest speed using the dough-hook attachment until a smooth dough is formed, adding the remaining water when necessary. Knead for at least 5–7 minutes or until the dough becomes shiny. Alternatively the mixing can be done by hand in a medium-sized bowl and then turned out on to a clean table and kneaded for 5–10 minutes until smooth and shiny.

Place the dough into a clean bowl which has a light coating of olive oil. Cover with cling film and leave in a warm place until it has doubled in bulk. Knead again gently to expel the excess air and cut into two. Sprinkle the table with a little flour and shape the dough into two sausage shapes approximately 25cm long.

Preheat the oven to 180°C/350°F/gas mark 4. Brush a heavy baking sheet with olive oil and lay the loaves on this keeping them well apart. Brush the top and sides of the loaves carefully with the remaining egg. Cover the loaves with cling film and leave in a warm place until they have risen approximately half again in size.

Place the loaves on the middle shelf of the oven and raise the temperature to 190°C/375°F/gas mark 5. This will assist in the immediate rising of the dough before the heat forms the crust. Bake until crisp and golden, approximately 25–30 minutes, by which time the bread will sound hollow when the base is knocked. Cool and use within 2 days.

Parmesan Bread Toasts

half a Parmesan loaf (see 204), preferably a day old

Preheat the oven to 160°C/325°F/gas mark 3.

Slice Parmesan bread as finely as possible and bake for 5–8 minutes or until crisp and golden. Cool before serving.

GRILLED TURBOT, MARINATED PEPPERS, OLIVES & PARSLEY WITH POTATO-CHIVE PANCAKE

This dish requires last-minute cooking and assembly but is well worth the effort as it looks very appealing, and as turbot is my favourite fish this is one of my favourite recipes. The rösti-style potato pancake may need a little practice to perfect, but with care, by following the directions, the careful turning of the potato should allow it to all end up back in the pan! The confident cook may try to turn the half-cooked pancake over with a plastic spatula in one go, but I do not recommend this method for first-time rösti makers.

For the marinated peppers, olives and parsley

3 red peppers
2 cloves garlic, crushed to a cream with a little salt
approximately 100ml olive oil
250g herb-marinated black olives, pitted and roughly chopped
½ bunch of chives, cut in 1cm lengths
2 tbsp leaves of Italian flat-leaf parsley
salt and pepper

Cut both ends away from the peppers and retain for another use (e.g. soups). Cut the peppers into three or four straight-sided pieces, according to the shape of the pepper, and remove the seeds. Either preheat a grill or salamander to the highest heat and place the peppers on a tray skin-side up and grill close to the heat source until the skins blacken, or heat a barbecue or char grill to the highest heat and place the peppers skin-side down and cook until charred.

Place the peppers in a bowl and cover tightly with cling film to steam-cool. Peel away the charred skins and discard. Cut the pepper pieces into large triangular shapes approximately 2cm high. Place in a bowl with the remaining ingredients, tossing gently. Leave in a cool place.

For the potato pancake

1 kg large red-skinned potatoes, preferably Desirée, washed well, skin on
approximately 8 tbsp olive oil
salt and pepper
½ bunch of chives, chopped

Using a mandolin, or the large aperture on a vegetable grater, shred the potatoes.

In a non-stick pan, heat 4 tbsp of olive oil until smoking. Add the potato carefully and press down gently to flatten it evenly with a wooden spoon or heat-proof plastic spatula. Cook over a high heat for approximately 3–4 minutes or until the base is crisp, golden and firm, adding a little extra olive oil if it becomes dry. Slide the potato cake on to a plate, invert another plate over the top, and turn them over carefully together. Add 4 tbsp more olive oil to the pan and heat, then slide the potato uncooked-side down into the pan and cook as before until crisp and golden. Alternatively, individual potato pancakes may be made by placing small piles of the grated potato in the hot oil and frying as before, using a plastic spatula to turn the potato when crisp. Season with salt and pepper and sprinkle with chives. Keep warm, uncovered, in a low oven.

For the turbot

olive oil
6 x 120g turbot fillet pieces, trimmed of bones and skin
pepper
6 lemon wedges
6 parsley sprigs

Preheat a char grill or griddle pan brushed with a little olive oil over a medium to high heat or heat a drizzle of olive oil in a non-stick frying pan.

Place the turbot pieces on a plate, skinned-side down, and smear with a little olive oil and sprinkle with pepper.

Place the turbot on the grill or griddle pan skinned-side up, at an angle to the bars or ribs, and allow to cook until the bar marks are golden. Turn over carefully and continue to cook on the other side. Alternatively place the fish in the preheated pan and cook until golden then turn as before. Depending on the thickness of the fillet this may take up to 2–3 minutes per side. To test for the doneness, press the fish lightly with a finger: if the texture is springy to the touch it is ready. Under no circumstances should the fish overcook as this will toughen the flesh and render it dry and unappealing to the palate. If the juices start to flow from the fish in the pan, it is almost too late, so remove it rapidly.

To serve, slice the potato pancake in wedges and place on 6 warm serving plates. Arrange the turbot on top, spoon over the red-pepper relish and garnish with lemon wedges and parsley sprigs.

POACHED AUTUMN FRUITS IN MARSALA & SPICES

1 bottle inexpensive sweet white wine, e.g. Jurançon
150ml Marsala or port
150g sugar
1 vanilla pod, split lengthwise
1 cinnamon stick
6 black peppercorns
peelings and juice of 1 orange and 1 lemon
250ml water
750g quinces
3 large ripe pears, Comice, Bosc or Conference
12 dried apricots
12 peeled chestnuts

TO SERVE
whipped cream or crème fraiche

In a heavy-based stainless-steel pan mix the sweet white wine, Marsala or port, sugar, vanilla pod, cinnamon stick, peppercorns, citrus peel and water, cover and simmer for 30 minutes. Strain, reserving the liquid, and the vanilla pod and cinnamon for the finished dish. Meanwhile wash the quinces very well to remove the 'down', then cut them into quarters and remove the peel and core. Sprinkle with the citrus juices. Place the quince and juices in a stainless-steel pan, cover with half the poaching liquid, cover with a disc of greaseproof paper and place a smaller lid on top so that the fruit remains submerged during cooking. Simmer very gently for 30–50 minutes or until the quince is tender and has turned a brilliant red-pink colour. Place the quince in a bowl, moisten with a little of the syrup and allow it to cool.

While the quince is poaching, quarter and peel the pears and poach them in the same way in the remaining liquid and excess quince poaching liquid, allowing 10–15 minutes. They should look almost translucent when cooked. Decant the pears into the bowl with the quince and moisten with a little extra syrup if necessary.

Place the apricots in the remaining fruit syrup with the chestnuts and simmer for up to 20 minutes or until they both just begin to collapse. Remove with a slotted spoon to the serving dish. Bring the syrup to a boil and pour over the fruits. Cut the vanilla pod into 3 and break the cinnamon stick into long shards and use these to decorate the dish. Serve warm or chilled with whipped cream or crème fraiche.

& AUTUMN

Bloody Mary

Spiced Nuts

Salad of Runner Beans, Figs, Rocket & Parmesan

Soup of Pumpkin Baked Whole with Parmesan,
Gruyère, Cream & Rosemary

Spiced Corn Soup with Chilies & Crème Fraiche

Carrot, Cumin & Coriander Soup

Ham, Vegetable & Bean Broth

Wild Mushrooms Baked in Cream, with
Gorgonzola Mascarpone

Baked Beans

Baked Lentils

Smoked Fish with Beetroot, Mustard Leaves
& Horseradish

Salad of Mussels with Tomatoes & Samphire

Braised Lamb Shank with Red Wine,
Orange Peel & Green Olives

Mashed Parsnips

Damson 'Soup' with Blackberries & Vanilla Ice Cream

Tarte Tatin

Watermelon Rind Pickle

B L O O D Y M A R Y

1.2 kg ripe or overripe red tomatoes
½ bunch (35g) of coriander, washed well
small sprigs of thyme, parsley and rosemary
20g fresh horseradish root, peeled and chopped small,
　　or 1 tsp prepared horseradish
juice of 2 lemons and 2 limes
1 tsp salt
2 cloves garlic, peeled
1 small red or green chili

TO SERVE
Maldon salt
vodka
lime wedges
celery hearts

In a liquidizer or food processor purée all the ingredients until smooth. Pass through a sieve, pushing the solids through well with the back of a ladle. Adjust the seasoning to taste. It should be spicy, salty and invigorating! Chill and serve without ice in tall glasses, sprinkled with Maldon salt, laced with vodka and accompanied by lime wedges and lots of heart of celery to cut the piquancy.

SPICED NUTS

A very special ex-member of staff, now living in Germany, sent me this recipe as she felt that it would be a perfect item to sell in the shop. She was right. In fact they have become so popular that we have to make enormous batches almost daily to keep up with demand.

200g mixed shelled nuts of your choice, almonds,
    hazelnuts, cashews, pistachios, pecans
1 tbsp chopped rosemary
¼ tsp cayenne
1½ tsp brown sugar
1 tsp salt
½ tsp creamed garlic
½ tsp walnut or olive oil

Preheat the oven to 160°C/325°F/gas mark 3.

Mix all the ingredients together and spread out over a baking sheet. Bake for 10 minutes, remove from the oven and stir the nuts, carefully turning them over. Continue to bake for a further 10 minutes. Allow to cool on the tray. You will want to eat them as soon as possible, but *if* there are any left over they will keep fresh stored in an airtight container for up to a week.

SALAD OF RUNNER BEANS, FIGS, ROCKET & PARMESAN

FOR THE BALSAMIC DRESSING

2 tbsp balsamic vinegar

6 tbsp olive oil

Maldon salt and pepper

1 small shallot, very finely diced

FOR THE SALAD

350g runner beans, tops trimmed and tails retained, washed and sliced on the angle

6 very ripe purple or green figs

good olive oil

salt and pepper

150g rocket leaves, trimmed of long stalks, washed and spun in a salad spinner

150g Parmesan, shaved with a sharp knife or vegetable peeler

1 tbsp long chopped chives

Mix the dressing ingredients together and leave them to infuse.

Bring a pan of salted water to the boil and add the beans, bring them back to the boil and cook for 1–2 minutes or until they have just lost their natural crispness. With a slotted spoon remove them to a tray or baking tin to cool quickly. (We rarely plunge green vegetables into iced water as it removes so much of the flavour.) Trim the tops off the figs and cut them into halves or quarters depending on the size. Chill 6 salad plates.

Place the beans in a bowl with a drizzle of olive oil and salt and pepper, toss together and divide between the plates. Place the rocket leaves into the same bowl with a little more olive oil, salt and pepper and toss gently. Arrange the leaves attractively with the Parmesan shavings and pieces of fig. Finally drizzle the balsamic dressing with a small spoon over and around the salad and scatter the chives. Serve immediately with Thyme & Maldon Salt Breadsticks (page 192) and the remaining dressing separately.

SOUP OF PUMPKIN BAKED
WHOLE WITH PARMESAN, GRUYÈRE,
CREAM & ROSEMARY

While I was living in California I met many gifted people who were to shape my life in one way or another. One of them was Deborah Madison who, along with Edward Espe Brown, conceived a brave new Zen-inspired restaurant. Theirs was the first real vegetarian restaurant in America which served thoughtfully prepared dishes from organically grown vegetables, salads and herbs. It was far from a hippie restaurant serving beans and rough wholemeal bread, but a San Francisco restaurant of style and confidence, with twenty-foot-high windows overlooking the Bay. It spawned many a courageous cook who followed their good example. Deborah and Edward co-wrote the inspirational *Green's Cook Book* in 1987, which I have spent much time reading and re-reading.

This is one of their dishes which has been plagiarized often, but I am about to do the same – with a few alterations.

This dish is perfect to offer at an informal lunch or supper as it is both warming and fun to serve. But one word of warning – it is very filling. I once served it to my family as a first course to precede another dish but everyone instead decided to finish the meal simply with fruit and coffee.

Ideally serve it with hunks of crusty bread followed by a crisp salad of cos lettuce heart, celery and watercress.

1 pumpkin weighing approximately 2 kg, preferably round, not oval
250ml double cream
100ml single cream
2 cloves garlic, crushed
salt and pepper
1 tsp chopped rosemary leaves
80g Gruyère cheese or mature Cheddar, grated
120g Parmesan shaved with sharp knife or potato peeler
rosemary sprigs and parsley sprigs

Preheat the oven to 180°C/350°F/gas mark 4. Wash the pumpkin well, slice off the stalk end approximately a quarter of the way from the top, and retain it. With a strong-handled spoon scoop out the seeds. Place the pumpkin in an ovenproof serving dish just large and deep enough to hold it and to support its lower half. In a pan heat the double and single cream with the garlic, salt, pepper and rosemary. Pour into the cavity and replace the lid.

Bake it in the oven for 1–1½ hours, depending on the density of the flesh. Take it out of the oven and carefully remove the lid. The flesh should feel tender enough to scoop with a spoon. Sprinkle the Gruyère or Cheddar cheese into the cavity and reduce the oven to 160°C/325°F/gas mark 3. Return to the oven with the lid half covering the top and continue cooking for 10 minutes.

Serve at the table in 6 flat soup plates, giving each portion a scoop of the flesh and a ladleful of cream. Garnish with Parmesan shavings and sprigs of rosemary and parsley.

SPICED CORN SOUP WITH CHILIES & CRÈME FRAICHE

60ml olive oil
2 medium onions, sliced
4 sticks celery, chopped
1 head fennel, chopped
6 heads fresh corn, kernels removed from the cobs
1 tsp salt
3 cloves garlic, chopped
1 chili, chopped
a few coriander stalks, plus 2 tbsp chopped coriander leaves

FOR THE GARNISH
2 heads corn, kernels removed
30ml olive oil
½ chili, very finely chopped
salt
1 tbsp chopped coriander leaves
120ml crème fraiche
6 coriander sprigs

In a heavy-based pan heat the olive oil with the onion, celery and fennel and stir until the vegetables start to absorb the oil. Add the corn, salt, garlic, chili, water to barely cover and coriander stalks and stir until well mixed. Bring to a boil and simmer with the lid on for 30 minutes or until the vegetables are soft. Purée in a food processor or liquidizer until smooth and push through a sieve into a clean pan. Add the chopped coriander leaves and taste for seasoning.

For the garnish, sauté the corn in a small pan with the olive oil and chili. Season with salt and add the chopped coriander. Pour the hot soup into 6 bowls and divide the corn garnish between them, piling it into the centre. Add crème fraiche and finish with a sprig of coriander.

CARROT, CUMIN & CORIANDER SOUP

60ml olive oil
3 cloves garlic, crushed
1 small red chili, cut in half
3 tsp cumin seeds
2 tsp coriander seeds
750g carrots, peeled and cut into large chunks
2 large onions, peeled and cut into large chunks
4 sticks celery, washed and cut into chunks
1 medium fennel bulb, washed and sliced
approximately 700ml water
2 tsp salt
1 large bunch of coriander, washed, 6 sprigs picked,
*   stalks removed from remaining leaves*

TO SERVE
120ml soured cream (optional)

Over a medium heat in a heavy-based pan warm the olive oil with the garlic, chili, cumin and coriander seeds until the spices begin to sizzle and the aroma is released. Turn up the heat, add the vegetables and stir well to coat each piece with the flavoured oil. Cover with a lid and cook without colouring for 4–5 minutes, stirring occasionally. Add water to barely cover, and salt and the coriander stalks. Bring to the boil, cover and simmer until all the vegetables are soft, approximately 20 minutes. In a food processor or liquidizer, purée almost the entire contents of the pan, retaining a little of the liquid in case the soup is too thin. It can always be added at the last minute but is impossible to remove once it is part of the soup. Push the soup through a sieve into a clean pan. Chop the coriander leaves and stir into the soup, taste and adjust the seasoning. Serve hot or chilled with a scoop of soured cream, a sprig of fresh coriander and chili-coriander focaccia (made as page 53, omitting the thyme and adding 1 small chili, chopped finely, and 1 tbsp chopped coriander).

HAM, VEGETABLE & BEAN BROTH

This broth can easily be made without the ham if preferred.

150g dried white beans, soaked overnight in cold water
1 x 700g piece of San Daniele ham hock or similar
1 onion, peeled, left whole, root on
2 celery stalks, broken in half
1 large carrot, peeled and cut in half
3 bay leaves
4 tbsp olive oil
1 clove garlic, crushed to a cream with a little salt
1 tsp chopped winter savory or rosemary
1 tsp chopped thyme
2 medium carrots, peeled and cut into small dice
2 stalks celery, cut into small dice
1 medium onion, cut into small dice
1 leek, white and pale green parts only, sliced thinly and washed
2 tbsp picked Italian flat-leaf parsley leaves
2 tbsp picked pale green celery leaves

Drain the beans and place them in a large stainless-steel pan, cover them with water and bring to the boil. Strain and return to the cleaned pan with the ham hock, onion, celery, carrot and bay leaves. Cover with three times their volume of water, bring to the boil, skim and simmer until the beans are tender, approximately 1–1½ hours according to the variety chosen. On no account should the beans remain al dente. They must be cooked well. Add salt to taste if necessary and leave the beans to cool in the broth. Remove the vegetables and reserve for another use (for example as a simple cold salad cut into small chunks tossed in herbs and olive oil). Drain the beans and ham hock and reserve the liquid.

Meanwhile, in a heavy-based pan, heat the olive oil with the garlic and herbs.

Add the diced vegetables and stir over a high heat until the oil is absorbed and the onion has turned translucent. Do not allow the vegetables to colour. Add 1½ litres of the bean liquid and bring to the boil. Simmer for 15–20 minutes or until the vegetables have become soft. Add the beans and the leeks to the vegetables and continue to simmer for another 5–10 minutes or until the flavours have amalgamated to your taste. Meanwhile, trim the ham hock of excess fat and rind and slice thinly with a sharp knife. Add this to the broth and finally stir in the parsley and celery leaves and serve.

WILD MUSHROOMS BAKED IN CREAM WITH GORGONZOLA MASCARPONE

My mother is the best golfer I know, but in the autumn months her game goes seriously downhill. I am sure that she hits the balls into the woods on purpose though, because more often than not she can be found emerging from the bushes with her golf bag filled to the brim with ceps, bay boletus, hedgehog mushrooms and other forms of fungi.

Once home, we trim them together, eliminating any maggots, and then I ask one of the restaurant's official wild mushroom suppliers to verify their authenticity. We then place them on the menus in recipes such as this. Its flavours speak volumes to me of why this season is so special.

NB Do not attempt to search for and cook your own mushrooms unless you know a mushroom expert who is able to authenticate your harvest for you. Alternatively make a study of one of the authorized books on the subject (see *A Passion for Mushrooms* by Antonio Carluccio or *Mushrooms and other Fungi of Great Britain and Europe* by Roger Phillips).

600g wild mushrooms, brushed and trimmed of discoloured parts
50g butter
2 cloves garlic, crushed to a cream with salt
salt and pepper
2 tbsp chopped Italian flat-leaf parsley, and 6 sprigs for garnish
2 tsp chopped fresh rosemary, and 6 sprigs for garnish
450ml double cream
60g Gorgonzola mascarpone

Preheat the oven to 180°C/350°F/gas mark 4.

Cut the mushrooms into large even-sized pieces. Heat the butter in a heavy-based non-stick frying pan, add the garlic and when sizzling add the mushrooms. Toss over a high heat and cook until almost tender. Season with salt, pepper, parsley and rosemary and remove with a slotted spoon to an ovenproof dish. To the remaining juices in the pan add the cream and reduce by a third. Taste for seasoning and pour over the mushrooms. Bake for 10–15 minutes or until the cream has bubbled and started to brown at the edges. Scoop Gorgonzola mascarpone into walnut-sized pieces, dot it over the mushrooms and allow it to melt as it is served. Garnish with sprigs of parsley and rosemary.

BAKED BEANS

400g dried beans, soaked in cold water overnight
3 bay leaves
1 whole onion, peeled
2 stalks celery, broken in half
½ fennel, left whole
140ml olive oil
1 medium onion, diced
2 stalks celery, cut small
½ fennel, cut small
2 carrots, peeled and cut small
3 cloves of garlic, crushed
1 tbsp chopped sage
500g ripe or overripe tomatoes, chopped roughly
2 small red chilies, chopped roughly
½ tsp salt
200g day-old plain bread
2 cloves garlic, crushed to a cream with salt
1 tsp chopped sage
1 tbsp chopped Italian flat-leaf parsley
salt and pepper

Drain the beans, place them in a large pan, cover them well with water and bring them to the boil. Strain and rinse. Return the beans to the pan, cover well with fresh water, and add the bay leaves, whole onion, broken celery, and fennel. Bring to the boil and simmer until tender throughout. This will take approximately 1–1½ hours depending on the variety of bean chosen. On no account must they be al dente as they can be very indigestible and the result somewhat embarrassing. Allow them to cool in the broth and then strain, reserving the liquid. Preheat the oven to 160°C/325°F/gas mark 3.

Meanwhile, heat 60ml olive oil in a heavy-based pan and add the onion, celery, fennel, carrot, garlic and sage. Cook until lightly coloured, then add the tomato, chili and salt. Add 500ml of the strained bean cooking juices and simmer until the vegetables are very tender, approximately 20 minutes. Strain the contents of the pan through a wide-gauge sieve and taste for seasoning. It should be spicy and have a distinct tomato flavour. Place the beans in a clean pan and add the sauce. Simmer over a gentle heat until the beans have started to absorb the liquid but still have a soupy consistency.

Meanwhile make the breadcrumb topping. Trim away most of the crust of the bread and cut it into walnut-sized pieces. Process in a food processor until medium fine, or use the liquidizer in small batches. Heat the remaining olive oil in a heavy-based non-stick frying pan and add the breadcrumbs. Stir continually over a medium heat until the crumbs become crisp and golden. Remove from the heat, and add the garlic, herbs, salt and pepper.

Pour the beans and sauce into a deep ovenproof dish and spread the crumbs over evenly. Bake for 30–45 minutes or until the sauce has bubbled up around the sides and become crusty.

BAKED LENTILS

Puy lentils from central France are ideal for this recipe. They are fine, full of flavour and hold their shape well even after long cooking. From Umbria come the more expensive Castelluccio lentils, which are even prettier as their mixed colours range from yellow to orange to gold to amber. They are slightly smaller in size but also work beautifully for this recipe.

This recipe for Baked Lentils is very similar to Baked Beans (page 224) but has the advantage of being prepared within an hour or two, as the lentils do not require presoaking. Serve with grilled or roasted meats or on its own with a salad of various leaves as a light vegetarian supper dish.

FOR THE LENTILS
60ml olive oil
1 onion, finely diced
2 carrots, diced small
3 celery sticks, diced small
2 cloves garlic, crushed to a cream with 1 tsp salt
1 tsp chopped rosemary
2 bay leaves
300g Puy or Castelluccio lentils
1 small red chili, finely chopped, with seeds
500ml fresh tomato juice
1 litre cold water

FOR THE CRUST
200g plain white or brown or herb loaf, preferably 1 day old
80ml olive oil, plus a little for drizzling
1 clove garlic, crushed to a cream with salt
1 tbsp chopped parsley
1 tbsp chopped coriander
Maldon salt and pepper

In a heavy-based stainless-steel pan heat the olive oil with the onion, carrot, celery, garlic and herbs. Stir over a medium heat until the onion has begun to soften. Add the lentils and continue to cook until they are well coated in the flavoured oil. Add the chili and tomato juice and cover with the water. Simmer for approximately 15 minutes or until the lentils are almost tender, adding a little water from time to time if they begin to look dry.

Meanwhile make the breadcrumb topping. Preheat the oven to 160°C/325°F/gas mark 3. Trim away most of the crust of the bread and cut into walnut-sized pieces. Process in a food processor until medium fine, or use the liquidizer in small batches. Heat the olive oil in a non-stick frying pan and add the breadcrumbs, stirring continuously over a medium heat until crisp and evenly golden. Remove from the heat and add the garlic, herbs, salt and pepper.

Pour the lentils into an ovenproof dish, draining a small amount of liquid away if it looks too soupy. Scatter the breadcrumbs over the top, drizzle with olive oil and place on the top shelf of the oven for 15–20 minutes or until crusty and sizzling.

SMOKED FISH WITH BEETROOT, MUSTARD LEAVES & HORSERADISH

1kg beetroot, preferably baby or small
2 tbsp olive oil, plus a little for drizzling
Maldon salt and pepper
1 tbsp balsamic vinegar
150g fresh horseradish or 1 tsp of prepared horseradish
300ml double cream, lightly whipped
juice of 1 lemon
150g salad leaves, if possible red mustard, mizuna, wild rocket,
*   landcress, watercress*
400g smoked salmon, thinly sliced
300g smoked eel, filleted and sliced on an angle
dill sprigs and long chopped chives
lemon wedges

Scrub the beetroot well and simmer it in salted water until tender, approximately 20–30 minutes, depending on size. Cool and peel under running cold water. Trim the tops and tails away and halve or quarter them depending on the size. Toss in the olive oil, salt, pepper and balsamic vinegar. Leave to marinate. Peel, grate and chop the horseradish finely and mix with the cream, then season and add the lemon juice. Do not overmix as it will stiffen quickly.

Place the leaves in a salad bowl, drizzle with olive oil, add salt and pepper and toss gently.

Arrange the smoked fish on one side of salad plates and place the leaves attractively to the other side. Place the beetroot carefully in the centre, as the colour will bleed into the other ingredients, and sprinkle with the dill and chives. Finish the plate with a lemon wedge and a spoonful of the cream.

SALAD OF MUSSELS WITH TOMATOES & SAMPHIRE

Some very dear friends who have a lovely house in the Rousillon area of France invited me to stay for a few days one summer. We shopped in the Carcassonne market all morning and came home with their car brimming with lovely cheeses, fruits and mussels. I had no idea how I was going to prepare the mussels until I started cooking, but then the recipe started to fall in place. I steamed the mussels in a little leftover white wine and picked them out of the shell. I washed and picked over the samphire (marsh asparagus) and cut the baby red tomatoes in half. The mussel-cooking liquor was reduced by half by boiling rapidly and mixed with olive oil. All the ingredients were tossed together with chopped basil and thyme, then chilled and laid on a platter. Good crusty baguette from the local baker helped to soak up the lovely juices.

BRAISED LAMB SHANK WITH RED WINE, ORANGE PEEL & GREEN OLIVES

One of the most popular items we serve on our autumn and winter lunch menus is a lamb shank, braised in red wine, herbs and garlic. Braising is an ideal way of cooking meats which tend to be tough, as it is a slow, gentle method requiring a certain amount of liquid to enhance the flavours and to assist in the tenderizing. To some customers, the whole shank arriving at the table seems rather daunting as it looks large and perhaps a little gauche. But the bone content is almost fifty per cent of the total and therefore it is not as filling as expected. The meat is juicy and tender and will if cooked correctly fall off the bone, but only just. The

orange juice in the recipe adds acidity and sweetness, aiding the syrupy quality of the reduced sauce.

60g unsalted butter, heated and allowed to settle, then strained through muslin
6 lamb shanks, trimmed of excess fat or gristle
1 large onion, peeled and cut into quarters
2 large carrots, peeled and roughly chopped
4 sticks celery, roughly chopped
1 small fennel, washed and roughly chopped
1 leek, trimmed, halved, washed and roughly chopped
6 cloves garlic, crushed
1 spray each of rosemary, thyme, bay and sage
peelings and juice of 2 oranges (approximately 250ml)
½ bottle hearty red wine
750ml Light or Dark Chicken Stock (pages 39 and 40)
240g green olives
salt and pepper

Preheat the oven to 160°C/325°F/gas mark 3. In a heavy-based ovenproof pan with a lid heat half the clarified (strained) butter and seal the lamb shanks over a medium heat on all sides until they turn golden. This may take up to 15 minutes. Remove to a bowl. Add the remaining butter and cook the vegetables and garlic over a high heat until they begin to colour. Add the herbs, orange peelings and juice, lamb, red wine and chicken stock. Season and stir well together, bring slowly to the boil, skim, cover with a lid and braise in the oven for 1 hour or until the meat has begun to recede from the shank bone and is tender. It may be necessary to check the pot from time to time to make sure that the liquid is only bubbling very gently. Carefully remove the shanks to a shallow ovenproof dish, cover and leave on one side. Strain the juices into a clean pan and boil rapidly to reduce by half, skimming occasionally to remove the impurities or fat which may rise to the surface. Add the green olives and taste for seasoning. Pour the juices over the shanks, cover and reheat gently for 20 minutes in the oven before serving.

MASHED PARSNIPS

1.2 kg medium-sized parsnips, peeled and cut into even-sized pieces
200 ml milk
salt
bay leaf
50g unsalted butter
pepper

Place the parsnips in a pan and half cover them with water. Add the milk, salt and bay leaf and cover and simmer until the parsnips are tender. Drain and keep the juices. Mash the parsnips with a little of the cooking juices using a potato masher, or place in a food processor for a smoother purée. Add butter, salt and pepper and serve.

DAMSON 'SOUP' WITH BLACKBERRIES & VANILLA ICE CREAM

This is not really a soup in the classic sense but could be seen as a sweet version of the Soup of Five Tomatoes & Three Beetroots (page 113) in as much as it is a purée of the main ingredients, served chilled in a soup plate decorated with whole fruits and a scoop of vanilla ice cream. If mulberries are available, they make a lovely addition to this dessert.

1 kg damsons
¼ bottle inexpensive red wine, Beaujolais or other light style
150g sugar
1 cinnamon stick
300g blackberries
100ml sweet white wine or sugar syrup
Vanilla Ice Cream (see over)
6 sprigs mint
icing sugar

Wash the damsons well and place them in a stainless-steel pan with the red wine, sugar, cinnamon stick, and water to barely cover. Cover and simmer gently until the fruits are very soft. Remove the stones, which will have risen to the top, and push the remaining contents of the pan through a plastic or stainless-steel sieve with the back of a ladle, pressing as much of the solids through as possible. Taste and check the consistency. It should have the thickness of a puréed soup. Chill.

Cook the blackberries in a stainless-steel pan with the sweet wine or sugar syrup for 2–3 minutes, taste for sweetness and add a little sugar if required. Cool.

To serve, divide the damson 'soup' amongst 6 soup plates and place 1 large scoop of vanilla ice cream on top of each. Arrange the blackberries over the top, decorate with a sprig of mint and dust with icing sugar.

V ANILLA I CE C REAM

1 vanilla pod
80g sugar
250ml milk
4 egg yolks
250ml double cream

In a food processor, grind the vanilla pod with half the sugar. Place the milk in a pan with the vanilla sugar and bring very slowly to a simmer. Allow to infuse off the heat. Whisk the egg yolks with the remaining sugar, adding the milk until well blended. Return the liquid to the pan and place over a low heat, stirring continuously with a wooden spoon until the custard starts to thicken and coat the back of the spoon. Strain through a fine-meshed sieve into a bowl and place this bowl over a bowl of iced water to cool the custard rapidly. Add the cream and churn in an ice-cream machine according to the manufacturer's instructions.

T ARTE T ATIN

There is only one way to make a Tarte Tatin and this is it. It is not an easy process and it may take two or three disasters before you perfect the art, but once it is done, you will thank Clarke's for ever for giving away the secret of success! Unfortunately it does require a lot of elbow grease afterwards to render the stove top spotless again, but it is well worth it.

Choose firm, fresh eating apples, preferably Golden Delicious or Jonagold, of equal size and ripeness. A scrupulously clean heavy-based sauté pan, approx-imately 24 cm across, preferably non-stick with a steel handle, is essential.

150g butter, soft but not oily
125g caster sugar
2 kg firm eating apples, Golden Delicious or Jonagold
400g puff pastry or sweet pastry (page 124) or brioche dough (page 148)

TO SERVE
crème fraiche

Using your fingertips spread the butter over the surface of the pan like a paste, as evenly as possible, leaving a clean rim at the top of approximately 1 cm. Sprinkle over the sugar as evenly as possible and leave in a cool place. Peel the apples whole, cut in half from top to bottom and remove the core carefully with a small sharp knife or melon baller. Do not worry if the apples start to discolour whilst doing this.

Place the apple halves around the inside rim of the pan, standing them upright, stalk end up, gently pressing them into the butter and sugar to keep them firmly in place. As each piece of apple is placed make sure that it is inter-locking with the next so that the inside of each apple covers the outside of its neighbour. Continue with a tight ring of upright apple halves inside the first ring, finishing with a half or two quarters to fill the gap in the centre. The result must be a very tightly fitted pan of apples without a space to move. Next place the two or three remaining halves on the top. These will be placed in later to create an even tighter fit.

Roll out the pastry or brioche dough to approximately 3cm wider than the diameter of the pan and leave in a cool place. Preheat the oven to 200°C/400°F/gas mark 6. Place the pan over a high heat and cook the apples until the butter and sugar begin to caramelize and the apples start to soften. Turn down the heat a little if the apples start to burn before softening, and increase it if there seems to be a lack of colour to the apples and too much juice overflowing from the pan covering the cooker top in a sticky caramel. The trick here is to start caramelizing the apples whilst at the same time evaporating off some of the excess juices as the fruit starts to soften. From time to time turn an apple half towards the centre of the pan to check the amount of colour on the base. As the apples cook they will soften and this will enable the extra halves to be inserted into the apple configuration with the help of a small knife or fork. This must be done with extreme care, with the heat turned down, as the caramel can burn fingers very easily.

Once the majority of the apples are a medium gold the tarte is ready for the oven.

Remove the pan from the heat and cover the apples with the prerolled pastry or brioche dough. Tuck the excess pastry around the edge down in between the apples and the pan. Make one large incision in the centre to allow the steam to escape during cooking, place it on a baking sheet, to catch the drips, and then put it in the oven. Bake for 20–25 minutes or until the pastry or brioche dough is crisp and golden. Remove from the oven and allow to cool for a few minutes. With a firm hand wrapped in a thick oven cloth, grasp hold of the pan handle. With the other hand also protected with a cloth, place a serving dish upside down over the top of the pan. Pressing the pan and the plate firmly and securely together, tip the pan upside down over the plate, allowing all the juices from the pan to arrive on the plate with the tarte.

If the apple halves have slipped a little during landing, rearrange them gently with a small knife. Eat as soon as possible with lots of crème fraiche.

WATERMELON RIND PICKLE

Thank you to Stephanie Alexander in Melbourne, for allowing us to use this recipe from her book *Menus for Food Lovers* (Methuen Haynes, 1985).

Makes 5 x 340g jars

1 x 2 kg watermelon, washed well
75g salt
1 litre water
1 kg sugar
600ml white wine vinegar
600ml water
1 lemon, thinly sliced
2 sticks cinnamon, broken roughly
1 tsp whole cloves
1 tsp allspice berries

Cut the watermelon into wedges and slice most of the flesh away from the skin, leaving approximately 2cm of flesh attached. The flesh will stay fresh in the fridge for 2–3 days and can be used for sweet or savoury salads or just by itself. Cut the rind into short strips and soak them overnight in the salt and water.

The next day drain them and place them in a heavy-based pan, cover with fresh water and simmer for 30 minutes or until tender. Drain. Make the pickling syrup by simmering all remaining ingredients for 10 minutes. Add the rind and boil rapidly until transparent, approximately 30 minutes. Meanwhile preheat the oven to 180°C/350°F/gas mark 4. Lay the scrupulously clean jam jars on a baking sheet and sterilize in the oven for 10 minutes. Boil the lids in a small pan of water for 5 minutes to sterilize. Bottle immediately and store in a cool dark place for at least a month before using. It will last for up to 1 year.

Serve with cold sliced meats, hard strong cheeses, or just straight out of the jar!

WINTER

TRUFFLES

When truffles arrive in the kitchen, either black or white, the cooks get excited and the office gets worried. Whatever time of the year, whatever the weather conditions in France or Italy, truffles are an exorbitant price. Over the years however, truffles have been found in such far-flung places as Wales and China, the latter apparently being cultivated, although the experts in France dispute the authenticity of this. To them the growth of the black truffle is shrouded in mystery, some say in witchcraft, and could never be imitated.

But to those who love the genuine article, its aroma, its look, texture and feel, it's worth every penny.

The white truffle, found in late autumn in northern Italy, especially around the area of Alba, is surely that nation's gastronomic highlight. For the foragers who dig for them, an annual salary can often be earned in just one good season's work: the selling price to London restaurants in 1998 ranged from £1,200 to £1,800 per kilo depending on size and availability. These truffles normally arrive in England embedded in boxes of cold sand and there is no mistaking the smell as the box is opened. Because of their price and the fact that at Clarke's we are restricted to a menu price (I would never add a supplementary charge to cover an extravagance of this kind) white truffles are not often used at the restaurant, but when we do it is cause for celebration. They are used very simply, raw and with immediacy. The warmth of the dish on which the shavings of truffle sit is sufficient to draw the essence up to the nostrils. Either shaved raw over freshly cooked pasta ribbons with unsalted butter and Parmesan or over risotto made with chicken stock and saffron threads, I am not fussy, but for me the aroma is almost more pleasurable than the eating. I have wonderful memories of Harry's Bar in Venice as well as the London Harry's Bar during the autumn and winter months: both display, in the dining room, their thousands of pounds' worth of white truffles, in bowls of Carnaroli or Arborio rice, simply covered with a linen cloth just waiting to be chosen.

South-western France, particularly the area around Perigord, produces the majority of the coal-black truffles, and these were priced between £250 and £350 per kilo in 1998. Many of these truffles are sent immediately to canning factories where they are preserved in brine, but to me this process impairs their flavour and their texture is rendered as rubbery as a black olive which has been through the same ordeal. But the market for them is forever strong as many classic restaurants find it difficult to cook without truffles year-round. However, at Clarke's we tend to use them only from October to early spring when we can guarantee their freshness.

Sows were traditionally used for the foraging, as to them the scent of the truffle can easily be confused with that of an overexcited male pig. This explains why the sows are vociferous in their desperate search for the source of the scent, often forcing themselves headlong into the ground and devouring the black jewels in the process. It is therefore obviously up to the skill of the owner to prolong the search only until the prize is discovered, and to cease the digging just in time. But the pig has been almost completely replaced in both Italy and France, for reasons of their size, weight and pure force, by specially trained dogs, which have learned the characteristics of the smell and can search out the truffles with skill and remarkable ease. In a wonderful story the late eminent American food writer, M. F. K. Fisher, describes the skill of a virgin (of a certain age) who with the aid of her extremely long nose was able to do the same thing.

Once the truffles have been ordered and delivered to the restaurant, the most important first step is their weighing, as a miscalculated gram or two can send the restaurant's accounts department reeling. After the truffles are weighed, they are checked for firmness. If they feel at all soft it may well indicate the presence of a family of maggots. These soft truffles are immediately rejected. A careful check is also carried out that they are whole, as one trick of the foragers, which I have learned to my cost, is that some broken truffles (which are therefore less expensive) are occasionally skilfully skewered back together with a carefully concealed tooth pick. This is usually only discovered when the truffle is being sliced or chopped, when it has already been paid for and is therefore too late. When they have had a full inspection they are brushed with a short-bristled brush which is kept purely for the use of fungi and then they are stored.

There is no way of preventing the aroma of truffles being released, but there are ways of absorbing the aroma into other foods for other uses. For example, an airtight plastic box containing Arborio or Carnaroli rice is our favoured vessel in which to store the black or white truffles, as the grains of rice slowly absorb the pungent smell and the rice can then be used for making very special risottos. Alternatively, a bowl of raw eggs in their shell with a truffle nestled in amongst them and then wrapped in plastic can be used, as the porous shells will allow the aroma to filter in. Even after a few hours these eggs will make the best omelette.

LUNCH

Poached Guinea Fowl with Winter Vegetables,
Herbed Lentils & Salsa Verde

Cheddar Cheese with Oatmeal &
Honey Bread Baked in a Flowerpot

Warm Lemon Pudding with Whipped Cream
& Pistachio Wafers

POACHED GUINEA FOWL WITH WINTER VEGETABLES, HERBED LENTILS & SALSA VERDE

2 x 1.2 kg guinea fowls
3 litres Light or Dark Chicken Stock (pages 39 and 40)
6 medium carrots, peeled and trimmed
3 fennel, halved and trimmed
6 medium leeks, trimmed to 15 cm in length and washed well
6 stalks celery, trimmed and cut into 15 cm lengths

Trim the guinea fowls of excess fat and skin and remove the parson's noses and neck ends. Place in a heavy-based stainless-steel pan and cover with the chicken stock. Top up with extra water if not completely submerged. Bring to the boil, skim and simmer for 25–30 minutes. Add the carrots, fennel, leeks and celery and continue to simmer for 20 minutes or until the meat juices run clear when skewered through the thigh. Remove the guinea fowl carefully to a plate and allow to cool. Strain the broth, reserving the vegetables, and allow to cool. Skim away the excess fat then bring to the boil and reduce by half.

Remove the legs from the guinea fowl and remove the skin. Cut in half at the joint between the thigh and drumstick, and trim off the ends of the drumsticks and discard. Remove the breasts carefully from the carcass and cut each one in two on a slight angle. Bring the broth to a boil and taste for seasoning. Place the guinea fowl pieces in a shallow pan, and pour over the hot broth to half cover. Carefully cut the vegetables into large attractive pieces and arrange in the dish. Simmer gently for 3–5 minutes and serve with herbed lentils, salsa verde and mustard fruits.

HERBED LENTILS

300g Castelluccio or Puy lentils
2 bay leaves
1 tsp salt
75ml olive oil
1 clove garlic, crushed to a cream with salt
1 chili, finely chopped, with seeds
1 tbsp chopped coriander leaves
1 tbsp chopped parsley leaves
1 tbsp chopped chives

Place the lentils in a heavy-based pan with the bay leaves and salt and enough cold water to cover to twice their depth. Bring to the boil slowly and simmer for 12–15 minutes or until tender to the bite. They should not become soft nor remain al dente but should retain their form and a little firmness. Drain and rinse with cold water until the liquid runs clear. To serve, place the lentils in a shallow pan with the olive oil, garlic, chili, herbs and salt. Add a splash of water and heat gently for a few minutes. Taste and adjust the seasoning if necessary.

SALSA VERDE

3 tbsp roughly chopped parsley
2 tbsp roughly chopped celery leaves
1 tbsp roughly chopped mint leaves
1 tbsp finely chopped chives
1 tbsp capers, drained and chopped
120ml olive oil
1 green chili, chopped very fine
Maldon salt
2 tbsp balsamic vinegar

Mix all the ingredients together except the balsamic vinegar, cover and leave to marinate for at least 30 minutes. Add the balsamic vinegar, taste and reseason if necessary.

OATMEAL & HONEY BREAD
BAKED IN A FLOWERPOT

For 2 flowerpot loaves

110g rolled oatmeal, plus 30g for coating the loaves
50g oatmeal flour
425g strong white flour
10g salt
40g honey
15g fresh yeast or 7g dried yeast
75ml milk
up to 200ml warm water
10g melted butter for brushing the pot

Mix the first four ingredients together in a mixing bowl. In a small bowl mix the honey, yeast and milk together until smooth. On the slowest speed, using a dough-hook attachment, mix the liquid into the flours, adding the warm water slowly until a soft dough is formed. Continue to mix for 5–6 minutes or until the dough is smooth. Alternatively the mixing can be done by hand in a medium-sized bowl and then turned out on to a clean table and kneaded for 5–10 minutes until smooth. Place the dough in a clean bowl, cover with cling film and leave in a warm place until it has doubled in size. Remove from the bowl and knead again to expel the excess air. Brush the insides of two scrupulously clean flowerpots, approximately 15cm high, or two loaf tins, approximately 15cm x 13cm, with the melted butter. Divide the dough into two and shape into balls, then gently splash them with a little cold water or briefly run them under a slow-running tap. Immediately roll them in the remaining oats, place them in the pots and cover with cling film.

Preheat the oven to 180°C/350°F/gas mark 4. Leave the loaves to rise to almost half again in size.

Place the pots on the middle shelf of the oven and turn the temperature up to 205°C/400°F/gas mark 6. Bake for 40 minutes or until the tops have started to colour. At this point the bread will sound hollow when the base is knocked. Cool and use within 3 days. Serve with Cheddar or another strongly-flavoured cheese.

WARM LEMON PUDDING WITH WHIPPED CREAM & PISTACHIO WAFERS

What would British restaurants do without the annual influx of Australians and New Zealanders who arrive on our shores simply wishing to work hard, earn as much as possible and to increase their skills and knowledge at the same time? At Clarke's our experience has been that most have brought nothing but smiles, enthusiasm and endless amounts of energy – as well as this recipe. Whether they were brought up in the bush or the metropolis, it seems that they were all raised at their mother's knee on this wonderful, simple, quick and easy dessert. As the spoon is pushed into the pudding it will pass first through a soft soufflé-like layer of lightness then into a rich creamy lemon-curdlike base. Divine!

60g butter
240g caster sugar
zest of 2 lemons
130ml lemon juice
30g flour, sifted
3 eggs, separated
280ml milk

Preheat the oven to 160°C/325°F/gas mark 3.

In a food processor or mixing machine with a beating attachment cream the butter with half the sugar together until light. Fold in the lemon zest, juice and flour and then the yolks. Gradually add the milk to make a smooth batter. Whisk the whites with the remaining sugar and fold into the lemon mixture.

Pour into 6 small ovenproof pots or ramekin dishes and place them in a deep dish which will hold them snugly. Half fill the dish with hot water and place in the oven to bake for 30–40 minutes. They should be puffed and tinged with pale golden edges. Eat either straight from the oven or just warm with whipped cream on the side and pistachio wafers.

PISTACHIO WAFERS

a little melted butter and flour to line the tin
50g egg white
60g caster sugar
100g flour
150g unsalted shelled pistachio nuts

Preheat the oven to 180°C/350°F/gas mark 4. Brush a loaf tin approximately 17cm x 9cm with butter, then line with parchment paper or silicone wax paper then brush again with butter and dust with flour.

Whisk the egg whites and sugar together until a soft peak is formed at the end of the whisk. Fold in the flour and pistachios at the same time until well blended. Pour into the prepared tin and flatten gently with a wet spoon. Bake for approximately 30 minutes or until pale golden and firm to the touch. Store overnight.

Preheat the oven to 130°C/275°F/gas mark 1. With a sharp serrated bread knife, slice the loaf very finely. Lay on a baking sheet and dry in the oven until crisp, approximately 15 minutes. Serve within 2 days.

SUPPER

Black Olive Crostini
with Salad of Blood Oranges,
Red Onion & Landcress

Pot-Roasted Pigeon with
Parmesan Polenta & White Truffle

Panforte with Dried
& Fresh Fruits

BLACK OLIVE CROSTINI
WITH SALAD OF BLOOD ORANGES,
RED ONION & LANDCRESS

450g marinated black olives, pitted
2 tsp capers
1 clove garlic, crushed to a cream with salt
1 small red chili, chopped fine, with seeds
3 blood oranges, including the grated zest of 2 of the oranges
1 tsp chopped thyme
2 tsp chopped parsley leaves
approximately 90ml olive oil
Maldon sea salt, if required
1 small firm red onion
6 fine slices of plain bread, preferably Country Bread (page 130)
150g landcress or watercress, long stalks removed
  (approximately 2 bunches)
good olive oil for drizzling
salt and pepper

First make the black olive paste.

Chop the olives and capers medium fine, and add the garlic, chili, orange zest, thyme and parsley. Mix well together and moisten with olive oil until a smooth paste is achieved. Taste and add salt if desired.

Cut the top and root end from the red onion and peel the tough outer leaves of skin away. Cut it in half and then slice with a small sharp knife as finely as possible and rinse in a bowl of iced water, gently separating the slices from each other. Drain and spin in a salad spinner or dry on kitchen paper.

Peel the oranges with a small sharp knife, making sure that all the pith is removed also. Slice into fine slices, remove the pips, but keep the orange 'together' at this stage.

To serve, heat a grill or salamander to the highest setting and grill the bread on both sides until golden. Place the cress leaves in a bowl, drizzle with olive oil, season with salt and pepper and toss gently.

Place the toasts at an angle in the centre of each plate and spoon a little olive paste on to each one. Arrange the orange slices and landcress decoratively and scatter onion rings over the top.

POT-ROASTED PIGEON WITH PARMESAN POLENTA & WHITE TRUFFLE

6 squab pigeons
salt and pepper
3 tsp chopped thyme leaves
3 large carrots, peeled
1 large onion
4 sticks celery
1 fennel bulb
60g unsalted butter
1 head garlic, roughly chopped
½ litre hearty red wine
½ litre Dark Chicken Stock or Game Stock (pages 40 and 42)
4 bay leaves
a sprig each of rosemary, thyme and sage

Preheat the oven to 180°C/350°F/gas mark 4.

Trim the wing tips, neck end and parson's nose from the pigeons and dry the cavities with kitchen paper. Season the cavities with salt, pepper and thyme.

Chop the carrot, onion, celery and fennel into hazelnut-sized pieces.

In a large heavy-based pan over a medium heat, warm a third of the butter until sizzling. Place the pigeons in the pan, breast-side down, and turn them occasionally until the skin turns golden, about 8–10 minutes. Remove the pigeons to one side and add half the remaining butter to the pan. Over a high heat, cook the diced vegetables and garlic until golden brown, stirring occasionally to scrape the residue from the bottom of the pan. Arrange the pigeons breast-side up on top of the vegetables, season with a little extra salt and pepper and add the wine, stock, bay leaves and sprigs of herbs and bring to the boil. The liquid does not have to cover the birds completely.

Put a lid on the pan and place it in the oven. Cook for at least 25–35 minutes or until a skewer moves without resistance through the thigh meat. Remove the pigeons to a deep platter and cover with foil to keep them warm. Place the pan over a high heat and reduce the liquid by half, skimming frequently to remove any fat or scum which may rise to the surface. Strain the juices into a clean pan and taste for seasoning. Heat to a gentle simmer and stir in the remaining butter. Pour over the pigeons and serve.

PARMESAN POLENTA

700ml water
salt
black pepper
2 tsp chopped thyme leaves
150g medium-ground polenta
50g unsalted butter
100g grated Parmesan

TO SERVE
1 white truffle, approximately 30g (optional), brushed of sand

Bring the water to the boil in a heavy-based pan with the salt, pepper and half the thyme. Pour the polenta into the pan slowly and gently, whisking it continuously until it becomes smooth. With a wooden spoon, continue to stir it over a low heat as it thickens. This will take up to 15 minutes, during which time the polenta will cook through. Remove from the heat and add the butter, the remaining thyme and half the Parmesan. Taste, and serve sprinkled with the remaining Parmesan and shavings of the white truffle if using.

PANFORTE WITH DRIED & FRESH FRUITS

One of the attractions of the beautiful city of Sienna, set in the Tuscan hills, is in almost every shop window the appealing display of panforte. There are the traditional ones wrapped in paper decorated with ancient battle or biblical scenes or there are enormous slabs on view covered with crinkly rice paper and dusted with a thick layer of icing sugar ready for slicing. Some are flavoured with dark chocolate, some are more spicy than others, most are hard but there are some softer and more chewy for those who prefer it. A small slice is all that is necessary of this rich sweetmeat, heavily studded with nuts and dried fruits and intensely flavoured with honey and spices. It is perfect to serve as an alternative to a dessert, particularly in the colder months, with espresso coffee or a glass of vin santo or Madeira. Obviously it would be simpler to buy a ready made panforte, now easily available in Britain from most good Italian delicatessens, but the pleasure derived from creating this yourself, as the rich aromas fill your kitchen with images of Renaissance Italy, will be well worth the time and effort.

30g butter, plus a little for lining the tin
150g hazelnuts
150g sugar
200g honey
160g whole blanched almonds
150g candied orange peel, chopped
150g candied lemon peel, chopped
1 tsp lemon zest

45g flour
1 tsp cinnamon
¼ tsp grated nutmeg
¼ tsp ground coriander seed
icing sugar, for dusting

Preheat the oven to 180°C/350°F/gas mark 4.

Lightly butter a 20 cm springform tin and line with parchment paper. Lightly butter it again and line it with one layer of rice paper. If rice paper is not available, the parchment will work by itself.

Place the hazelnuts on a baking tray and roast for a few minutes or until the skins start to flake away. Gently rub them in a cloth to remove the skins. Over a low heat dissolve the sugar, butter and honey and then bring to a boil. Cook until it reaches the hard ball stage, 123°C/250°F. Immediately add all the remaining ingredients except the icing sugar and stir until well blended, then pour into the prepared tin. Reduce the oven temperature to 160°C/325°F/gas mark 3 and bake for 30–40 minutes or until the edges begin to set. Remove from the oven and allow to cool in the tin. It will set on cooling. Remove from the tin and dust heavily with icing sugar.

Slice and arrange neatly on a serving dish decorated with a selection of fresh and dried fruits such as clementines, pears, grapes, blood orange wedges, dried apricots, peaches, figs, and muscat raisins.

DINNER

GRANARY ROLLS WITH FOUR SEEDS

BUCKWHEAT BLINI WITH SMOKED SALMON
& CRÈME FRAICHE

GRILLED ROE DEER WITH CHESTNUT GLAZE;
SPICED RED CABBAGE & PARCHMENT-BAKED
ROOT VEGETABLES

SPENWOOD CHEESE WITH QUINCE PASTE
& OATMEAL BISCUITS

BAKED VANILLA CREAM WITH ARMAGNAC
PRUNES & GINGER FLORENTINES

GRANARY ROLLS WITH FOUR SEEDS

300g wholewheat flour
200g white flour, plus extra for dusting
1 tbsp sunflower seeds
1 tbsp pumpkin seeds
10g salt
10g fresh yeast or 5g dried yeast
1 tsp honey
300ml warm water
1 tsp sesame seeds
1 tsp poppy seeds

In a mixing bowl mix the flours, sunflower seeds and pumpkin seeds together with the salt. In a small bowl mix the yeast with the honey and half the warm water until smooth. On a slow speed, using the dough-hook attachment, mix the liquid into the mixing bowl, adding the remaining warm water slowly until a soft dough is achieved. Continue to knead until the dough is smooth and shiny. Alternatively the mixing can be done by hand in a medium-sized bowl and then turned out on to a clean table and kneaded for 5–10 minutes until smooth. Place the dough in a clean bowl, cover with cling film and leave in a warm place to prove. It should double in size within 1 hour, according to the temperature of the kitchen and the weather. Place the risen dough on a table, lightly dust with white flour and knead again to expel the air. Cut into 12 equal pieces and shape into short sausage shapes approximately 10cm long. Mix the remaining seeds in a small bowl and one by one turn the rolls over in the seeds until well coated, pressing the seeds in gently. Place the rolls seeded-side up on the baking sheet and cover with cling film.

Preheat the oven to 180°C/350°F/gas mark 4. Leave the rolls in a warm place until risen to half again in size, approximately 30 minutes. Place on the middle shelf of the oven, immediately turn the temperature up to 200°C/400°F/gas mark 6 and bake for 15–20 minutes or until the rolls are crisp and dark golden brown. Cool and eat within 2 days.

Alternatively, the mixture can be baked as 2 loaves. Simply shape the dough into 2 balls. Cover with seeds, as above, and allow to rise for 30–40 minutes. Bake at the same temperature, for 30–35 minutes.

BUCKWHEAT BLINI WITH SMOKED SALMON & CRÈME FRAICHE

70g buckwheat flour
85g flour
10g sugar
1 tsp salt
160ml milk
10g fresh yeast or 5g dried yeast
2 eggs, separated
1 tbsp chopped dill and 6 dill sprigs
100g clarified butter, warmed
salt and pepper
300g sliced smoked salmon (approximately 12 slices)
120ml crème fraiche

Mix the flours together with the sugar and salt in a bowl and create a well in the centre. Warm the milk to barely blood temperature, remove it from the heat and stir in the yeast and yolks and mix until amalgamated. Pour this into the well and gradually stir the flours into the liquids until smooth. Leave covered in a warm place for 1 hour or until it has doubled its bulk.

Mix the chopped dill with half the butter and season with salt and pepper. Keep in a warm place.

Whisk the egg whites until soft peaks are formed and fold gently into the batter.

In a wide flat non-stick heavy-based pan heat the remaining butter. Test a small drop of the blini mixture in the hot butter. If it sizzles immediately, it is ready to fry. Using a medium-sized ladle, make 6 individual blinis and cook until golden on the underside. Very carefully flip the blinis over with a plastic or metal spatula and cook the other side in the same way, trying not to allow the blinis to touch each other. Cook 3 at a time if it is easier and keep the first 3 warm whilst cooking the remaining ones. Sprinkle with a little salt and serve as soon as possible.

To serve, place a blini on each warm serving plate and drizzle with dill butter. Lay the salmon slices over the top in curls and spoon crème fraiche on top. Garnish with the dill sprigs.

GRILLED ROE DEER WITH CHESTNUT GLAZE

600g loin of young venison
½ tsp chopped thyme
½ tsp chopped rosemary
½ tsp chopped sage
2 cloves garlic, crushed to a cream with salt
½ tsp pepper
30ml olive oil

FOR THE SAUCE
50g unsalted butter
1 onion, peeled and chopped small
2 sticks celery, chopped small
2 carrots, peeled and chopped small
3 cloves garlic, crushed
½ tsp peppercorns
a handful of thyme, rosemary and sage stalks
½ bottle good hearty red wine
500ml Dark Chicken Stock or Game Stock (pages 40 and 42)
200g cooked and peeled chestnuts

Ask your butcher to trim the loin to the eye of the meat, thus removing all fat and sinew. (Some of the trimmings may be used minced for sausages or hamburgers.) Mix the herbs, garlic, pepper and olive oil together, rub this over the surface of the loin and leave it to marinate, covered, for up to 12 hours in the refrigerator.

For the sauce

Heat half the butter in a heavy-based pan until foaming. Add the vegetables, garlic, peppercorns and herb stalks and stir over a high heat until dark golden in colour. Add the red wine and stock, bring to the boil and skim. Keep the stock boiling gently, skimming frequently and reduce by two-thirds. The resulting liquid should be clear and glossy. Strain into a jug and cool.

Remove the meat from the fridge 30 minutes before cooking to bring it to room temperature and preheat a grill or griddle pan to a medium-high heat. Place the loin on the grill at an angle and seal for a few minutes. Criss-cross the loin by moving it 90° and grill again until for a few minutes. Turn the meat over and repeat the process on the second side and grill until well sealed. Depending on the thickness of the loin, this will take up to 6–10 minutes for a medium to rare result. The meat should feel firm on the outside but should give a little when pressed gently with a finger. Alternatively, the venison can be roasted. Preheat the oven to 200°C/400°F/gas mark 6, seal the meat with a little hot butter in a roasting tin, then roast for 5–8 minutes.

Remove the meat to a plate and cover. This will allow the meat to relax, giving the loin time to continue cooking a little but at the same time setting the juices inside. This will make the meat even more tender when it is ready for slicing.

To finish the sauce, skim away any fat from the surface and pour into a small pan, heat gently and taste. Over a low heat stir in the remaining butter, add the chestnuts and taste.

Slice the venison, arrange over the spiced red cabbage and place the parchment-baked root vegetable package next to it. Pour some of the sauce over and around the meat and serve the remaining sauce separately.

SPICED RED CABBAGE

500g red cabbage
1 small red onion
50g unsalted butter
45ml olive oil
1 small red chili, chopped fine
1 tsp chopped rosemary leaves
1 tsp salt
juice and zest of 2 oranges
75g raisins
1 tbsp chopped Italian flat-leaf parsley leaves
1 tbsp chopped coriander leaves
45ml balsamic vinegar (or good red wine vinegar)

Slice the red cabbage and red onion finely. In a flat pan with a tight-fitting lid place the butter and olive oil, and enough water to cover the base. Mix the cabbage and red onion together with the chili, rosemary and salt and place in the pan. Add the orange juice and zest and raisins and cover with the lid. Cook over a high heat, stirring or shaking the pan occasionally to allow the cabbage to cook evenly. If the pan becomes dry add a splash of water and cover again with the lid. The cooking will take no more than 8–10 minutes, as the cabbage should remain al dente. Remove from the heat, add the parsley, coriander and vinegar, taste and serve.

PARCHMENT-BAKED ROOT VEGETABLES

You will need 6 discs of silicone wax paper approximately 30 cm in diameter, and 6 pieces of string 20 cm long.

6 small potatoes, washed and peeled
3 medium parsnips, washed and peeled
½ celeriac, washed and peeled
6 shallots, peeled whole, hairs of roots trimmed
60g unsalted butter, melted
Maldon salt
pepper
1 tsp chopped thyme
1 tsp chopped rosemary
6 bay leaves

Preheat the oven to 180°C/350°F/gas mark 4.

Cut the potatoes, parsnips and celeriac into walnut-sized pieces and dry them by wrapping them in a clean tea towel. Place them in a bowl with the remaining ingredients and toss together to coat with the butter. Lay out the discs of paper and divide the vegetables evenly in the centres, using 1 bay leaf for each package. Gather the edges together carefully in a 'beggar's purse' shape and tie tightly with the string with one simple bow. Place the packages on a baking sheet and bake for 20–25 minutes or until the vegetables are tender – test by piercing with a wooden skewer through the bag. Place one on each plate and allow guests to open the package themselves to experience, first-hand, the aromas of the herbed, buttery vegetables as the string is untied.

BAKED VANILLA CREAM WITH ARMAGNAC PRUNES & GINGER FLORENTINES

FOR THE VANILLA CREAM
1 vanilla pod
50g sugar
650ml double cream
6 egg yolks

FOR THE ARMAGNAC PRUNES
18 dried prunes
200ml orange juice
100g sugar
100ml water
12 peelings of orange approximately 5cm long, blanched in boiling water for 1 minute
½ wineglass of armagnac or cognac

In a food processor, grind the vanilla pod with half the sugar then add it to the cream and bring it to the boil. Remove it from the heat, cover and allow it to infuse for at least 1 hour.

Beat the yolks with remaining sugar, bring the cream back to the boil and pour over the yolks, stirring well until blended. Pour back into the pan and cook over a low heat, stirring continuously with a wooden spoon until it begins to thicken and coat the back of the spoon. Pass through a sieve into a bowl and place this over a bowl of iced water to allow the custard to cool rapidly. Pour into individual ramekin dishes or small pots, cover and refrigerate overnight until set.

Soak the prunes overnight in half the orange juice. Next day, place the remaining juice in a pan with the sugar, water and blanched orange peel. Simmer for 10 minutes, then add the prunes and any remaining soaking juice and simmer for 15 minutes or until tender. Allow to cool, add the armagnac or cognac and stir well.

To serve, divide the prunes, the orange peelings and a little of the juice amongst the pots and serve with Ginger Florentines.

GINGER FLORENTINES

75g hazelnuts
35g unsalted butter
90ml double cream
60g sugar
100g flaked almonds
55g crystallized ginger, roughly chopped
30g sultanas
5g flour

Preheat the oven to 180°C/350°F/gas mark 4.

Place the hazelnuts on a baking sheet and roast for 5–10 minutes or until the skins start to flake away. Cool them then rub them gently in a cloth and discard the skins. Chop the nuts roughly.

Slowly bring the butter, cream and sugar to a boil then add all the remaining ingredients, mixing gently but thoroughly.

Spoon 12 tbsp on to parchment paper with lots of space to allow for spreading. Bake for approximately 8 minutes or until golden. Allow to cool a little and slide on to a cooling rack with a palette knife. Ideally, eat within 24 hours, but they will keep for up to 3 days in an airtight container.

&

Nancy's Egg Nog

Savoy Cabbage Soup with Black Truffles & Cream

Black Truffle, Potato & Gruyère Tartlet

Salad of Pears with Belgian Endives, Fresh Walnuts
& Mustard-Honey Dressing

Coleslaw

Mustard Mayonnaise

Honey-Roasted Belgian Endives & Parsnips

Roasted Celery, Fennel & Onion

Grilled Squid Salad with Seville Orange Dressing

Grilled Skewered Duck Hearts

Roasted Pork

Roasted Pork Sandwich with Mustard Mayonnaise
& Rocket

Venison Sausages

Frittelle (Spiced Marsala Cream Buns)

Apple Brown Betty

Seville Orange Marmalade

Mango Relish

Spiced Pineapple Chutney

NANCY'S EGG NOG

When I lived in Paris as a student in the late 1970s I met Americans en masse for the first time, which was for me both startling and fascinating. They were so confident and outgoing, with personalities so far removed from those of my safe circle of friends in the Home Counties. Although I spent my first few weeks at college observing them with my mouth wide open, many subsequently became lifelong friends. I have a great deal to thank them for, not least this recipe, which is the most perfectly warming and delicious alcoholic Christmassy drink, so rich it is almost a food in itself.

3 eggs, separated
75g sugar
¼ bottle whisky
⅛ bottle rum
250ml milk
250ml double cream, lightly whipped
grated nutmeg

Whisk the yolks and sugar until thick and golden, then gradually whisk in the whisky and rum and then the milk. Whisk the whites until soft peaks are formed and fold into the mixture with the whipped cream until blended. Pour into a glass jug and serve in tall glasses with grated nutmeg over the top. Take a taxi home or stay the night!

SAVOY CABBAGE SOUP WITH BLACK TRUFFLES & CREAM

500ml Vegetable Stock or Light Chicken Stock (pages 38 and 39)
500ml double cream
2 sprigs each of thyme, rosemary and sage
2 cloves garlic, crushed
Maldon salt and pepper
1 small black truffle, approximately 30g
1 small Savoy cabbage, unsightly leaves discarded
50g clarified unsalted butter, warmed
salt and pepper
1 tsp chopped thyme leaves

Bring the stock to the boil and add the cream, herbs and garlic. Simmer until the broth has reduced by a third, strain into a clean pan, and season with salt and pepper. Trim a very small amount from two opposite sides of the truffle and chop the trimmings finely. Add these to the broth and infuse over a very low heat or a pilot light. Meanwhile, remove the dark and medium dark leaves from the cabbage stalk and wash well. (The yellow heart can be used for Coleslaw, page 278.) Cut the leaves in half and remove the large vein, then cut each half into triangular pieces 4–5cm across.

To serve, bring a pan of salted water to the boil and cook the leaves briefly until they just start to lose their crispness. Warm 6 soup plates. Drain and toss the cabbage in the butter, salt, pepper and thyme. Gently heat the cream broth to a simmer, and taste. Divide the cabbage between the soup plates and pour over the cream. Shave the remaining piece of black truffle over the top and serve immediately.

BLACK TRUFFLE, POTATO & GRUYÈRE TARTLET

FOR THE SAVOURY PASTRY

200g plain flour

½ tsp salt

100g unsalted butter

1 egg

approximately 15ml chilled water

FOR THE FILLING

60ml olive oil

1 tsp thyme leaves

2 medium onions, halved and finely sliced

salt and pepper

300g small potatoes, scrubbed and cooked until tender in boiling salted water
*   then cut in half*

1 egg and 2 yolks

250ml double cream

30g chopped black truffle

100g grated Gruyère

¼ bunch of chives, chopped fine

1 small whole black truffle for shaving, approximately 50g (if affordable)

To make the pastry, mix the flour and salt in a bowl. Rub the butter into the flour until it resembles breadcrumbs. Whisk the egg briefly and add to the mix with enough water to form a smooth dough, kneading quickly but lightly. Wrap and chill in a refrigerator for at least 1 hour before rolling.

Meanwhile, in a heavy-based non-stick pan warm half the olive oil with the thyme leaves. Add the onion and stir until well coated with the oil. Cook over a high heat, stirring occasionally until soft and golden. Season with salt and pepper and pour into a sieve over a bowl and leave to drain. Discard the juices. Heat the

remaining olive oil in the pan and fry the cooked potato until crisp and golden. Drain as before and season with salt and pepper.

Either cut the pastry into 6 pieces and line 6 x 11cm fluted tartlet tins or line 1 x 24cm flan ring if preferred with it, and chill it for at least 30 minutes. Preheat the oven to 190°C/375°F/gas mark 5. Line the pastry cases with small discs of greaseproof paper and fill almost to the brim with baking beans. Bake for 15–20 minutes or until the pastry edges are golden. Carefully remove the paper and baking beans and bake again for 2–3 minutes or until the base of the pastry is cooked.

In a bowl whisk the eggs gently with the cream, and salt and pepper. Stir in the chopped truffle and leave to infuse. Spread the onion mixture over the cooked tartlet bases, scatter with the potatoes and sprinkle with the Gruyère. Carefully pour in the egg-cream-truffle mixture, scraping every last piece of truffle out of the bowl. Sprinkle with the chives and place in the oven, immediately reduce the temperature to 160°C/325°F/gas mark 3 and bake for 20–25 minutes, or 30–35 if making one large tart, or until the custard has puffed and set. Allow to cool for a few minutes before removing from the tins. Serve, preferably while still warm, shaving the black truffle, if using, over each serving.

SALAD OF PEARS WITH BELGIAN ENDIVES, FRESH WALNUTS & MUSTARD-HONEY DRESSING

FOR THE DRESSING
2 tsp Dijon mustard
2 tsp whole-grain mustard
150ml olive oil
15ml champagne wine vinegar
1 tsp honey
salt and pepper

FOR THE SALAD
600g fresh walnuts in the shell, or 150g shelled whole walnuts, halved
olive oil
salt and pepper
3 ripe Comice or Conference pears
6 heads Belgian endive (chicory)
a few Italian flat-leaf parsley leaves

Whisk the mustards together then gradually incorporate the olive oil until an emulsion is formed. Add the vinegar and honey and blend until smooth. Season to taste.

Preheat the oven to 180°C/350°F/gas mark 4. If using walnuts in the shell, crack them carefully and remove the kernels, keeping each half as intact as possible. Place them or the already shelled nuts on to a baking sheet, drizzle with olive oil, add salt and pepper and bake for 20–30 minutes or until crisp and golden. Cool.

Wash the pears and dry them carefully. Trim any unsightly outside leaves from the endive, slice across approximately 2cm thick on an angle and place in a bowl with the walnut pieces. Cut the pears into quarters, core them and cut each one in half lengthwise. Add to the bowl with a drizzle of the dressing. Toss very gently together and arrange on 6 salad plates. Drizzle with extra dressing and serve immediately.

COLESLAW

200g Savoy cabbage heart
3 large carrots, peeled
2 small red onions, peeled and cut in half
3 stalks of celery
100g sultanas or raisins
75g pecans, toasted in a medium oven at 180°C/350°F/gas mark 4 for 4–6 minutes
a small handful of Italian flat-leaf parsley leaves, chopped

TO SERVE
Mustard Mayonnaise (see below)
6 sprigs of Italian flat-leaf parsley

Shred the cabbage heart finely with a sharp knife. 'Peel' the carrot into long fine slices with a vegetable peeler, reserving the core for stocks or soups. Slice the red onion and celery finely and place them in a bowl with all the other ingredients. When ready to serve, add the mustard mayonnaise and toss gently but thoroughly together with the parsley. Serve with cold sliced poached ham or cold roasted beef or just by itself.

MUSTARD MAYONNAISE

1 egg and 1 egg yolk, organic or free range
½ tbsp Dijon mustard
1 tsp whole grain mustard
250ml vegetable oil
juice of ½ lemon
salt and pepper

Beat the egg and egg yolk together with a wooden spoon or whisk and blend in the mustards. Very slowly add the oil, beating continuously until a thick emulsion is formed. Add a little lemon juice, and continue adding the remaining oil. Season to taste and add more lemon juice if desired.

This will keep in a sealed container in a refrigerator for up to 4 days.

HONEY-ROASTED BELGIAN ENDIVES & PARSNIPS

12 small parsnips, peeled, tops and tails trimmed
6 medium-sized Belgian endives (chicory)
50g unsalted butter
60ml olive oil
1 tbsp honey
2 tsp chopped thyme
Maldon salt
pepper
1 tbsp chopped Italian flat-leaf parsley leaves

Preheat the oven to 180°C/350°F/gas mark 4. Bring a pan of salted water to the boil and cook the parsnips until they have just started to lose their firmness, approximately 10 minutes. Drain and place in a gratin dish or another oven-proof dish. Halve the endives or cut them lengthwise into four, depending on the size, remove as much of the bitter core as possible (without releasing the leaves) with a small sharp knife, and arrange the pieces neatly with the parsnips. In a small pan heat the butter, olive oil, honey, thyme and salt and pepper until bubbling and drizzle over the vegetables evenly. Roast for up to 20 minutes or until the vegetables have begun to caramelize and soften. Sprinkle with the parsley and serve immediately.

ROASTED CELERY, FENNEL & ONION

1 head of celery, cut to 15cm long, tough outer stalks removed, bases trimmed
2 bay leaves
3 heads of fennel, washed and cut in half lengthwise, outer leaf removed,
 bases and tips trimmed
6 small to medium firm onions, the hairs of the roots removed but the
 skin retained and the top quarter of onion removed
100ml olive oil
2 cloves garlic, crushed to a cream with salt
1 tsp chopped thyme leaves
1 tsp chopped rosemary leaves
Maldon salt
pepper
2 tbsp roughly chopped Italian flat-leaf parsley

Preheat the oven to 180°C/350°F/gas mark 4.

Cut the celery into sixths, retaining the root portion on each piece to keep the stalks intact. Wash well.

Bring a pan of salted water to the boil and add the bay leaves. Add the celery pieces and cook until al dente, approximately 4 minutes. Remove them with a slotted spoon and drain. Cook the fennel in the same way for approximately 3 minutes. Cook the onions last as they will taint the water, simmering them for 10–15 minutes or until a sharp knife or skewer pierces easily. Drain. Mix together all the remaining ingredients except the parsley and spread half of this over the base of an ovenproof pan or heavy roasting tin.

Place the vegetables on top, in attractive rows, the onions cut-side down, and spoon the remaining herbed oil over the celery and fennel. Place in the oven and roast for 15–20 minutes or until the vegetables have started to brown. Turn them all over gently and continue to cook a further 10 minutes. Scatter the parsley over the vegetables and serve.

GRILLED SQUID SALAD WITH
SEVILLE ORANGE DRESSING

1 kg small squid, body length approximately 15 cm
2 medium red onions, peeled
3 large oranges
juice of 1 Seville orange
a pinch of salt
1 small red chili, chopped fine, with seeds
60 ml olive oil
2 tbsp coriander leaves
a few celery sprigs, washed

To clean the squid

If your fishmonger is unwilling to clean the squid for you it can be done simply at home. Place the squid in a colander in the sink and gently pull the head end including the tentacles away from the body. Rinse with cold water. The squid will contain a long narrow piece of cartilage and some white jelly, which need to be removed and discarded. Wash the squid thoroughly under the cold tap, removing at the same time any loose film of skin. Dry the squid on kitchen paper. There is a small white 'eye' contained in the centre of the head which needs to be discarded. This pops out easily when squeezed. Rinse the head and tentacles and dry as before.

To make the salad

Slice the red onions in rings approximately 5mm thick, keeping each slice in one piece. Remove the peel from one sweet orange with a vegetable peeler and slice into very fine 'needles'. Remove the peel and pith from all the sweet oranges, and segment neatly, removing any pips. Squeeze the juice from the membranes. Bring

a small pan of water to the boil and blanch the orange peel 'needles' for a few seconds. Drain and refresh under cold water.

Mix the Seville and sweet orange juices together with the orange needles, salt, chili and olive oil.

If you have a grill or griddle pan, heat it to its highest heat and grill the squid on both sides until the bar marks are golden, approximately 2–3 minutes. Immediately remove them to a chopping board and slice them across in rings, place them in the bowl with the dressing and toss together. Grill the onion slices on both sides until golden brown and toss into the dressing, separating the onion rings from each other gently.

If you don't have a grill, slice the squid into 5mm rings, then heat a drizzle of olive oil in a heavy-based frying pan and over a high heat sauté the squid until firm to the touch, approximately 1–2 minutes. Remove to the dressing with a slotted spoon. Drain the juices from the pan and dry the base with kitchen paper. Separate the onion slices into individual rings and over a high heat, with another drizzle of olive oil, sauté the onion until tender. Add to the dressing and toss while still hot.

When cool taste for seasoning and fold in the coriander, orange segments and celery sprigs and serve.

GRILLED SKEWERED DUCK HEARTS

The biggest nightmare of any restaurateur must surely be Valentine's night. It is a well-known fact that a room full of 'gruesome twosomes' creates no atmosphere whatsoever as couples are generally only interested in each other. Some couples will arrive with very different agendas in mind, there is usually a row somewhere, sometimes tears, and occasionally a small box will be passed across a table and the couple will choose to leave early. So in order to make the evening as fun and as bearable for my staff as possible, we have each year devised a set menu of five courses, instead of the normal four, matched by five wonderful Californian wines. This has proved to be a great success, with some couples rebooking for the next year as they leave. This is despite (or maybe because of) the fact that the first course has for fourteen years been the same, Grilled Skewered Duck Hearts.

From year one at Clarke's I have enjoyed serving this particular dish on Valentine's night. To some people it sounds strange and almost ghoulish, but on tasting, it is very different. These hearts are surprisingly tender and juicy and the spicy marinade makes them a perfect starter served on a small dish, sizzling straight from the grill.

18–24 duck hearts, trimmed of their pipes and sinew
4 tbsp roughly chopped coriander
1 red chili, finely chopped, seeds included
½ tsp Maldon salt
150ml sesame oil
150ml olive oil
zest and juice of 1 lime

TO SERVE
sprigs of coriander
lime wedges

Soak the hearts in cold water for at least 1 hour. Drain and cut each one in half lengthwise. Rinse again in cold water and pat dry with paper towels. Thread them on to short wooden skewers, using at least 6 halves per skewer. Arrange side by side on a plate. Place the remaining ingredients in a bowl and mix well. Spread half the marinade over the hearts, turn the skewers gently in the marinade and leave in a cool place.

Preheat a grill to its highest setting or gently warm a griddle pan brushed with a little vegetable oil.

Place the skewers on the grill or griddle, sear them for a few seconds and turn them over. Cook for 1 minute or less until medium rare and serve immediately, spread with the remaining marinade and garnished with sprigs of coriander and lime wedges.

ROASTED PORK

1 onion, cut into large chunks
3 celery sticks, cut into large chunks
2 carrots, peeled and cut into chunks
½ head garlic, chopped
1–1.2 kg leg cut of pork – ask your butcher to score the rind of the pork
    into fine lines for you unless you have a very sharp knife yourself
90 ml olive oil
salt and pepper
1 tbsp mixed chopped rosemary, thyme and sage
sprigs of bay, rosemary and sage
½ tbsp flour
½ bottle red wine
500 ml Dark Chicken Stock (page 40)
1 tbsp honey

Preheat the oven to 180°C/350°F/gas mark 4.

In a roasting tin place the vegetables then the pork and pour the olive oil over and around the meat. Generously sprinkle the pork with salt, pepper and the chopped herbs and rub this into the scored rind and the underpart. Place the tin on the stove over a high heat and cook until sizzling. Add the sprigs of herbs and place in the oven. Roast for 30 minutes then turn the temperature down to 160°C/325°F/gas mark 3. Continue to cook for a further 40 minutes or until done. Test by inserting a metal skewer into the thickest part. The tip should feel very warm when removed after a few seconds. Remove the pork from the pan to a carving board or dish and cover to keep warm while you make the gravy. Place the roasting pan back on a medium heat and skim away a little of the excess oil. Sprinkle with the flour and stir constantly, scraping the darkened vegetables away from the pan. Add the red wine and the stock and simmer until the gravy thickens and colours. Taste and add salt and pepper if necessary. Finally add the honey, return to the boil and strain. Use the leftovers for Roasted Pork Sandwich with Mustard Mayonnaise & Rocket (page 290).

ROASTED PORK SANDWICH WITH MUSTARD MAYONNAISE & ROCKET

Obviously this sandwich can easily be made on thickly sliced fresh bread for a more filling dish, but this interpretation is designed to be not only fun to look at but at the same time enticing and light to eat.

1 loaf of Granary Bread with Four Seeds (see page 257) or similar
leftover Roasted Pork (page 289)
approximately 3 handfuls of wild rocket leaves or watercress
olive oil
salt and pepper
Mustard Mayonnaise (page 276)
juice of 1 lemon

TO GARNISH
gherkins and caper berries or dill pickles

Preheat the oven to 150°C/300°F/gas mark 2.

Slice the bread as finely as possible (we use the ham slicing machine) and lay 12 slices on a baking sheet. Bake them for 5–8 minutes or until they have started to dry and curl upwards.

Slice the roasted pork wafer thin and leave in a cool place. Place the rocket or watercress in a bowl and drizzle with a little olive oil and salt and pepper and toss gently. Mix the mayonnaise with enough lemon juice to make it the consistency of double cream. Assembling the sandwiches gently, as the bread will now be very fragile, place a slice on each plate and arrange half the rocket leaves on top. Place the pork over this, spooning a little mustard mayonnaise over. Top with the remaining leaves and the remaining slice of toast and serve with gherkins and caper berries or dill pickles.

VENISON SAUSAGES

I have a lovely friend living in Scotland whose wonderful father-in-law once carried a carcass of his own venison in a cardboard box straight through the restaurant in the middle of dinner service. Thankfully no customer noticed but the following week the menus were filled with various dishes containing the delicious meat. Towards the end of the week, we were getting to the 'trimmings' and I decided to make sausages. When I told him over the telephone that I had done this, he practically had a fit. He could not believe that his special venison had been used to make something as ordinary as sausages. He never did let me forget about his wounded pride as a result of my disrespectful act.

However, these are far from ordinary sausages and can be made with most meats.

1kg boneless venison or lamb shoulder
200g boneless pork or veal shoulder, with a generous fat content
   (especially if using venison)
1 medium red chili, chopped fine, including seeds
Maldon salt
2 tsp fennel seeds
grated zest of 2 oranges
2 cloves garlic, crushed to a cream with salt
1 tsp chopped thyme
1 tsp chopped rosemary
1 tbsp chopped coriander leaves
1 tbsp chopped parsley leaves

Ask your butcher to grind the meats on a medium to fine setting or use the mincing attachment on a mixing machine. Place the meat in a large bowl with the other ingredients and mix well. Cover and keep in a cool place for up to 12 hours to marinate.

Test the mixture for seasoning by frying a walnut-sized piece in a little olive oil, and adjust if necessary. Form into sausage shapes using a dusting of flour if the mixture becomes sticky. At the restaurant we do not use sausage skins, instead we simply cook the sausage naked, like a hamburger. Grill or pan-fry them until the juices run clear when a skewer is pushed into the centre. Serve them with buttery mashed potato with a generous amount of mustard stirred into it, or Mashed Parsnips (page 231) or Parmesan Polenta (page 255).

FRITTELLE (SPICED MARSALA CREAM BUNS)

Makes 12 buns

In Venice, in celebration of Epiphany, almost every baker on every street is found to be frying these delicious little spiced buns throughout the cold weeks. In order to stay warm as one walks along the canals, it is imperative to make a pit stop once in a while to purchase a hot cup of frothy cappuccino and a frittella to go with it. Often the pastry cream which fills these buns is flavoured with vanilla, but I prefer the ones which have the added shot of Marsala, which results in an extra inner glow as one continues the promenade.

300g flour
½ tsp ground cinnamon
½ tsp mixed spice
a pinch of salt
50g butter
15g fresh yeast or 7g dried yeast
150ml warm water
50g caster sugar
1 egg yolk
100g lightly roasted blanched almonds, chopped
150g raisins

Sieve the flour and mix with the spices and salt. Rub in the butter. Dissolve the yeast in the water and add the sugar. Add this liquid to the flour, then the egg yolk and mix to form a soft dough. Add the almonds and raisins and either knead by hand for at least 10 minutes or until smooth and shiny, or use a mixing machine with a dough-hook attachment (this will take 3–4 minutes). Cover and leave to prove in a warm place until it has doubled in bulk, approximately 30–40 minutes. Knead again briefly and shape into 12 balls. Place on a lightly floured tray and cover them. Prove again until they have doubled in size (20–30 minutes). Preheat a deep-fat fryer to 170°C/338°F and fry, turning once, until golden in colour, approximately 5–6 minutes. Drain very well on kitchen paper, split and fill with Zabaglione Cream (see page 174, Zabaglione Cake with Strawberries).

APPLE BROWN BETTY

Apple Brown Betty is one of my very favourite desserts. It should consist of the sharp, acidic but buttery apple purée topped with the crisp sweetened spiced crumbs.

FOR THE TOPPING
50g butter
150g fresh breadcrumbs
50g brown sugar
2 tsp ground cinnamon
1 tsp mixed spice

FOR THE APPLE
1.6kg Bramley apples, peeled, cored and roughly chopped
150g sugar
25g butter

TO SERVE
whipped cream or crème fraiche

Heat the butter in a shallow heavy-based pan. Add the breadcrumbs and stir continuously over a medium-high heat as they become crisp. When they have turned golden remove them from the heat and stir in the sugar and spices. Allow them to cool.

Place the apples in a heavy-based stainless-steel pan with a splash of water and the sugar. Heat gently, cover with a lid and stir occasionally. A smooth purée with a few lumps will result after 10–15 minutes. Remove from the heat, stir in the butter and taste for sweetness, although the apples should retain most of their inherent sharpness.

Serve the warm apple in warm bowls sprinkled with a generous amount of crumbs and lots of whipped cream or crème fraiche.

SEVILLE ORANGE MARMALADE

To make approximately 5 x 500 g jars

6 Seville oranges
1 sweet orange
1 lemon
granulated sugar

With a sharp knife score the rind of all the fruit, making 4 vertical incisions, quartering the pith and peel of each one. Remove the pith and peel and slice this into shreds as finely as possible with a sharp knife. Squeeze the juices into a measuring jug. Place all the debris in a muslin bag and tie with a piece of string.

Add cold water to the fruit juices to measure 2 litres in total and place in a large bowl with the shredded fruit and the muslin bag. Leave to soak in a cool place or refrigerator overnight.

The following day pour the contents of the bowl into a large stainless-steel pan and simmer gently for 30–35 minutes or until the liquid has reduced by a small amount and the peel begins to look transparent. Cool and pour into a bowl and leave in a cool place overnight.

Remove the muslin bag from the bowl and squeeze all the juices from it into the bowl of fruit. Weigh the fruit and juice mixture: three-quarters of this weight will be required in sugar. Place the weighed sugar in a heavy-based stainless-steel pan, pour the liquids over and gently bring to the boil. Simmer for 1 hour, skimming away any scum which rises to the surface. Test the set by placing a small amount of the marmalade on a chilled saucer. It should have a jellied appearance after a few minutes in the refrigerator. Meanwhile preheat the oven to 180°C/350°F/gas mark 4. Lay the scrupulously clean jam jars on a baking sheet and sterilize in the oven for 10 minutes. Boil the lids in a small pan of water for 5 minutes to sterilize. Pour the marmalade into jars and screw on the lids firmly. This marmalade will keep for up to 3 months in a cool place.

MANGO RELISH

During our winter months other parts of the world are enjoying warmer weather and as a consequence we are able to import fresh exotic fruits such as mangoes and papayas from South America and pineapples from the Ivory Coast. It makes a refreshing change to be able to diversify once in a while and use these fruits in a restaurant which is usually firmly fixed to its European seasons.

This amount will be perfect for 6–8 people

3 large medium-ripe mangoes
juice and grated zest of 3 limes
¼ tsp salt
1 red chili, very finely chopped, with seeds
1 bunch of coriander, washed, stalks removed and leaves roughly chopped

Peel the mangoes with a small sharp knife and slice off the two flat sides as close as possible to the seed. Then slice off the two smaller sides. Dice the flesh as neatly as possible and place it in a bowl with all the remaining ingredients except the coriander leaves. Scrape the remaining flesh from the seed, chop finely and add to the relish. Leave to marinate for at least 2 hours in a cool place. Just before serving fold in the coriander.

Serve with grilled chicken or tuna, or with sirloin steak which has been rubbed with garlic, chili and coriander before grilling.

Spiced Pineapple Chutney

Makes 5 x 500g jars

1 small to medium pineapple, peeled and cut into 2cm chunks
300g dried apricots
500g Bramley apples, peeled, cored and cut into 2cm chunks
500g sliced onion
500ml champagne vinegar or white wine vinegar
500ml white wine
500g light brown sugar
1 large chili, chopped
2 tbsp yellow or brown mustard seeds or both mixed
1 tbsp salt
180g raisins
1 tbsp mint, chopped

Place the pineapple, apricots, apple and onion in a heavy-based pan with the vinegar and wine and simmer for 15–20 minutes. Add the sugar, chili, mustard seeds and salt and continue to simmer for 1 hour, or until it has reached a thick syrupy consistency. Meanwhile preheat the oven to 180°C/350°F/gas mark 4. Lay the scrupulously clean jam jars on a baking sheet and sterilize in the oven for 10 minutes. Boil the lids in a small pan of water for 5 minutes to sterilize. Add the raisins to the chutney and cook for a further 10 minutes. Remove it from the heat, stir in the mint, and bottle it, screwing the lids on firmly. This will keep for up to 1 year in a cool, dark place.

INDEX

CLARKE'S RESTAURANT
124 Kensington Church Street
London W8 4BH
Telephone 020-7221 9225
Monday to Saturday Lunch & Dinner
12.30 to 2 & 7 to 10 pm

& CLARKE'S SHOP
122 Kensington Church Street
London W8 4BH
Telephone 020-7229 2190
Monday to Friday 8am to 8pm
Saturday 9am to 4pm

& CLARKE'S BREAD WHOLESALE 020 -7221 7196